MW01309019

SECOND CHANCES

HOME TO  HEATHER CREEK

SECOND CHANCES

Leslie Gould

Guideposts

Home to Heather Creek is a trademark of Guideposts.

Published by Guideposts Books & Inspirational Media
100 Reserve Road, Suite E200
Danbury, CT 06810
Guideposts.org

Cover by Lookout Design, Inc.
Interior design by Cindy LaBreacht
Additional design work by Müllerhaus
Typeset by Aptara, Inc.

ISBN 978-1-959634-53-9 (hardcover)
ISBN 978-1-959634-57-7 (epub)
ISBN 978-1-959634-54-6 (epdf)

Printed in the United States of America
10 9 8 7 6 5 4 3 2 1

Acknowledgments

My thanks to the residents and staff at Courtyard Senior Living in Portland, Oregon for inspiration in what it's like to thrive in a senior setting. I'd also like to acknowledge the soccer fans in my life for exposing me to the thrills of the English Premier League, and the soccer players in my life, specifically my four children, for years of excitement as I've watched them play. Thanks also to my husband, Peter, for his encouragement and support concerning my writing and life in general.

—Leslie Gould

Home to Heather Creek

Before the Dawn

Sweet September

Circle of Grace

Homespun Harvest

A Patchwork Christmas

An Abundance of Blessings

Every Sunrise

Promise of Spring

April's Hope

Seeds of Faith

On the Right Path

Sunflower Serenade

Second Chances

SECOND CHANCES

Chapter One

The morning light cast a golden hue across the milking room. Charlotte breathed in the scent of the musty hay mixed with the dustiness of late August and rested her head against Trudy's side as the last ping of milk zipped down the side of the stainless-steel pail. "There, there, girl," she whispered. "I'm all done." She patted the cow's flank and then swung the pail, the white frothy milk lapping at the rim, to the other side of the stool.

"Grandma?" Christopher stood in the doorway of the barn. "May I help with the milking?"

"I just finished." Charlotte stood and smiled at her grandson. "You're up early." The rising sun shone behind his head.

"Yep." Christopher wore denim shorts and a blue T-shirt, and his blond hair stuck up at the crown of his head.

"Are you excited about your first day of sixth grade?"

He shrugged. "Did Emily talk with you?"

"About . . . ?" Charlotte carried the pail carefully.

"This morning." Christopher swung the door open wide for his grandmother.

Charlotte tilted her head as she stepped into the last cool moment of the day. Already it was obvious that another scorcher was in the works.

"Emily said that you and she had talked about today," Christopher said, stepping ahead of his grandmother.

Of course Emily had talked relentlessly about today, her first day as a sophomore at Bedford High, for the last several days. She'd gone over what she planned to wear this Monday morning. How she planned to fix her hair. How she and Sam were going to go early so they'd have time to organize their lockers, a motivation that was believable for Emily but hardly for Sam. Charlotte was sure his motivation was to hang out with Arielle.

"What in particular are you referring to that Emily talked to me about?" Charlotte asked.

"That she'd walk me into my class."

"Oh," Charlotte said as she closed the barn door. "But I'm taking you to school."

"That's just it," Christopher said. "I can ride with Sam and Emily. You can have the morning to yourself."

Emily hadn't said a word about taking Christopher to school. Charlotte's grandson took the pail from her, and a little milk slopped over the edge, falling on his sneaker. He didn't notice and started walking.

"Careful," Charlotte said. Did the kids, well, Emily, think she needed a morning to herself? Granted, things had been busy with the wheat harvest and the fair and the nonstop activity of the farm and the kids. And to be honest, Charlotte *was* looking forward to a little downtime, but she had always loved driving the kids, her own kids and her grandkids a year ago, to school on the first day. She liked the fresh clean smell of the school and seeing the students dressed in their new clothes. She knew she couldn't walk Emily and Sam into their classes—no one did that in high school—but she could still take Christopher for his first day of sixth grade and check in with his teacher, show her that he was well loved and cared for.

Christopher switched the pail to his left hand.

"I'll take you into school," Charlotte said.

"No, really, it's okay, Grandma." He switched the milk back to his right hand. "I don't need you to."

"But I want to," Charlotte said.

"Emily said you'd rather stay home and have some time to yourself."

Charlotte shook her head. "No, Christopher. I'm going to take you to school." It was typical of Emily to think she knew best.

Christopher shrugged again and a little bit more milk sloshed. "Well, talk to Emily. She had it all planned out."

Charlotte sighed. Emily was ready to run the family, if she'd let her. Well, she wasn't ready to give up the first day of school, no matter how much she longed for some time to herself. That would come soon enough. Last year Sam wasn't driving so it hadn't been an issue. This year everything was different.

Christopher switched the pail to his other hand. "Here," Charlotte said, reaching for the milk. "Let me take it the rest of the way."

He transferred the handle to Charlotte and then stepped ahead of her and began jogging toward the house. Toby ran out to greet Christopher, yipping and running behind him and then back out front. The boy swayed from side to side, teasing the dog, and then picked up a stick and lobbed it toward the field, stretching his body high. It looked as if Christopher had grown during the night. Soon he would be as tall as Charlotte.

A magpie flew up out of the high grass on the other side of the garden and then swooped down on a fence post, keeping an eye on the dog.

The purple pom-pom dahlias were in bloom and heralded the last days of summer. She stopped a moment, feeling the strain of the handle pressing against her hand. The pink snapdragons perfectly complemented the red, orange, and yellow lilies. She'd intended to cut a bouquet of flowers for something. What was it? Not the dining room table—Emily had put together an arrangement after church yesterday.

That was it. During church, Pastor Nathan had asked the congregation to think of ways they could bless the residents at Bedford Gardens Convalescent Center. He suggested bringing something in to brighten the place or stopping by to visit or play a game with a resident. Charlotte had decided on a bouquet of flowers, and she thought she might as well drop the bouquet by after she took Christopher to school.

"Christopher!" Emily stood at the back door, her hands on her hips. "Hurry! We don't want to be late." She'd straightened her hair until it looked like straw, and she wore a denim pencil skirt and two layers of tank tops. Charlotte hoped Emily planned to wear a blouse on top of them and save her from suggesting it.

Toby, with the stick in her mouth, approached Christopher, and the two wrangled for it until Christopher won and lobbed it toward the garden. The magpie squawked and took off, up onto a branch of the black walnut tree.

"Christopher!"

"Grandma's taking me," he called out, looking over his shoulder at his sister.

Charlotte picked up her pace and cut across the lawn. "Why don't you ride with me too, Emily? In fact, I don't think Sam should drive today. You can all go with me."

Emily shook her head. "Remember, we planned to go early."

Charlotte followed her granddaughter into the farmhouse, trying to remember if her own children had gone by themselves to high school on the first day. She put the milk on the worn countertop and then headed back outside, grabbing her garden shears from the shelf in the mudroom.

"Go get your breakfast," she called out to Christopher, stepping onto the back porch. "There's oatmeal on the stovetop and bacon warming in the oven."

"I'll take some oatmeal." Charlotte's son Pete sauntered toward the house, his baseball cap pulled down against his peeling, sunburned ears. Charlotte had given up hope that at thirty-five he'd start wearing sunscreen. "I'm starving," he said, rubbing his dusty hands on his jeans.

"What have you been up to?"

"Fixing the gate on the north quarter. I bumped it with the combine the last day of wheat harvest and finally got around to taking care of it." He turned toward Christopher. "I'll race you to the house."

"Pete." Charlotte's voice was shriller than she meant it to be, but it did the trick. He stopped and turned toward her. "Did you and Bill and Denise drive yourselves to high school on the first day, you know, when you were old enough to drive?"

Christopher stepped closer at the sound of his mother's name.

"I did." Pete pulled his cap off his head and ran his fingers through his thick hair. "I think Denise did too. But you probably drove Bill—which explains everything." Pete began to laugh and then poked Christopher and took off toward the house, yanking his hat back on his head as he ran.

Charlotte shook her head and started toward the garden. As she cut the dahlias she counted the years ahead. One more year until Sam left for college. Three more years for Emily. And seven more years for Christopher. Tears filled her eyes. What was wrong with her? She was sixty-five years old. She'd be seventy-two when Christopher left for college. Practically an old woman. No wonder she felt a little melancholy; life was speeding right along.

A HALF HOUR LATER, Charlotte pulled her Ford Focus into a parking space next to the elementary school. As she walked with Christopher toward the building she turned toward the high school across the street, hoping to catch sight of Emily or Sam. They'd left the farm quite a while before she and Christopher had. Was that Sam on the steps? And Arielle beside him? The first bell rang and the two started toward the door.

"Grandma." Christopher tugged on her hand. "Hurry."

Sam and Arielle disappeared into the high school, and Charlotte insisted that Christopher stop in front of his school as she pulled her old camera from her purse. He stood straight as an arrow with a serious look on his face. She clicked the shutter. "Now smile," she said, and he gave her a goofy grin. She clicked again, and then followed Christopher through the double doors of the elementary school, down the hall to his classroom.

"Bye," Christopher said as they entered the room. He slipped through her arm as Charlotte gave him a half hug.

"Do you have the check for the lunchroom?" she asked.

He nodded, slipped among the desks, and shot his grandmother a helpless look as he stopped next to the desk of Natalie Johnson.

"I'm Miss Luka," a young woman with short blonde hair said, extending her hand. She looked all of twenty-two, at the very most. "What is your son's name?"

"Grandson." Charlotte liked the sweet young woman already. "Christopher Slater. I'm Charlotte Stevenson." She smiled warmly.

"So nice to meet you," Miss Luka said. "I'm looking forward to a great year."

As Charlotte slipped through the door of the classroom and back down the hall, the sting of tears surprised her. She quickly swiped at her eyes. What was wrong with her? She had a whole day—a whole school year—ahead of her without having to deal with hungry, bored, or bickering kids for most of the day. She could work in peace, embroider, even start a new quilt if she wanted to.

She hurried out into the late summer sunshine and slumped into the seat of her car. Why did she feel so sad? A vague feeling of regret overcame her. It was all mixed up in feeling as if her nest was emptying, again. A mini empty nest, to be sure, because none of them were leaving for good, not yet.

She recalled feeling the same way when her children were still at home. What was it about the start of the school year? Most of the time she was happy with the direction her life had taken, but every once in a while she regretted not having done something more with her life, something meaningful. Like college and a career. She sighed as she shifted into reverse. When she graduated from high school though, marrying Bob had seemed like the most important thing in the world. And it wasn't that it hadn't been important. It had been. And it wasn't that she regretted it. Not really. How could she? She wouldn't have the life she had if she hadn't married Bob when she was nineteen.

She pulled out onto Lincoln Street and then slowed as she turned left on Main Street. Maybe she should stop by Fabrics and Fun after she was done at the nursing home. No, it was too early for Rosemary to be in her shop yet and just as well. She couldn't very well tell her sister-in-law that she regretted getting married forty-six years ago. Charlotte chuckled at herself. She was being ridiculous. She'd be fine by noon.

What she needed was a plan. Just for today. She would treat herself to a cup of coffee at Mel's Place after she dropped off the flowers. Then she would go home and sit down and make a list of everything she'd been putting off because she'd been going full steam ahead all summer. She would put washing the windows, cleaning the curtains, and thoroughly scrubbing the bathrooms on the list. She would put updating the horses' vaccines on the list. She would put making plum jam on the list and start picking the fruit this afternoon, before the plums all fell off the tree and became ammunition for Christopher to hurl across the fence.

Charlotte pulled into the parking lot of Bedford Gardens Convalescent Center. The vinyl siding needed to be washed, the trim painted, and the flower bed by the front door needed to be weeded. All these years later, she was still so relieved that her mother-in-law, Ma Millie, had never had to live there.

She shifted into park and turned off the engine. She hadn't been inside the nursing home for years. A couple of months ago, Rick Barnes had reported that the center had been sold and in addition to the nursing home and acute-care ward, the new owners were also remodeling to offer a few assisted-living apartments, which sounded like a needed addition, but still she shuddered. Charlotte hoped that she and Bob would never have to live here. She hoped that Bill and Pete and the grandkids would see to that. She sighed, wondering whether, if Denise had lived, she would have ever moved back home . . . if she would have come home to care for her parents in their old age.

Charlotte took a deep breath. Boy, was she on a roll this

morning with her "what-might-have-beens." She'd better snap out of it; it did no good to think this way. She swung her door open, shuffled around to the trunk, and wrestled the container of dahlias, lilies, and snapdragons to the pavement.

STANDING NEXT TO THE RECEPTION DESK was a woman with silver hair pulled back in a tidy bun and wearing a blue linen skirt and a perfectly pressed white blouse. When she saw Charlotte, a smile spread across her face and her blue eyes sparkled. "Oh, deary," she said with a slight British accent. "Lilies! My favorite flower." The woman took a step forward. "And dahlias and snapdragons. Flowers from the end of summer. How splendid! Who are they for, deary?"

"For everyone," Charlotte answered. "For whoever wants them."

The woman's pale blue eyes grew big, and she put out her hand to Charlotte. "I'm Ruth. Ruth Blake, but please call me Ruth." She turned toward the reception desk and called out, "Stephanie, we have a visitor, and she's brought more flowers with her."

Charlotte followed Ruth's gaze. A young woman sat behind a desk. She stood slowly, revealing a very pregnant belly. She put her hand to the small of her back as she stepped forward. "You must be from the church," she said.

"Yes," Charlotte answered.

The woman wore a cotton maternity dress and flat sandals. "You're the third person to bring in flowers—I'm running out of vases."

"Never mind that," Ruth said. "I have a plethora of vessels in my room. And no one's brought in lilies yet."

Stephanie smiled and said sheepishly, "Thank you. I guess Ruth will help you."

Ruth leaned against the counter. "Deary, I'm worried about you. Are you feeling all right?"

Stephanie began to massage her lower back with the ball of her hand. "It's this heat, that's all. I'm fine."

"Go home and put your feet up," Ruth said. "We can manage without you for a day."

Stephanie smiled at the old woman. "I'm fine, really."

As Charlotte lugged the bucket and followed Ruth toward the open staircase she noted the bouquets of flowers in the lobby. Roses and zinnias and daisies. They were beautiful. She hadn't been the only one to think that flowers would brighten up the dingy eggshell-colored walls and worn draperies. A water mark stained the far corner of the lobby ceiling.

"Oh, dear," Ruth said. "We'd better take the elevator." She turned toward the edge of the lobby. "I try to take the stairs as much as I can, but I don't want you to lug that heavy bucket any farther than you have to." She pushed the UP button for the elevator, and it opened immediately.

"Don't you just adore this time of year," Ruth said, pushing the 2 button. "The hot days. The harvest. The thunderstorms."

Charlotte agreed, guessing that Ruth probably felt the same about autumn, winter, and spring too. She seemed like that kind of a person.

The elevator door opened. "My apartment is down here," Ruth said and then lowered her voice. "It's only a studio—hardly qualifies as a home—but I was so happy to heal enough to be out of the nursing-care wing, to be fine and dandy again, that I don't mind how small it is."

"What were you healing from?" Charlotte asked.

"Oh, I had a problem with my hip and then a little heart trouble. That's all." Ruth slowed as they turned to the right, past a bald-headed man sitting at a table working on a jigsaw puzzle. The lid of the box showed a photo of a village of white buildings, a church in the middle, alongside a blue river with green, green grass all around.

"Top of the morning to you, Ruth," he said.

"Good morning, Red. I'm pleased to introduce Charlotte to you."

Red stood slowly, holding on to the chair for support and rose to his full height, which was several inches shorter than Charlotte. He held out his hand and said, "I'm always pleased to meet a pretty lady, a lady nearly as lovely as Ruth."

Ruth shooed him away. "Oh, Red. No one believes a word you say." But she blushed a little as she continued down the hall. "I have one of the new assisted-living units," Ruth said. "And so does Red. The other ones haven't been rented out yet." A moment later she unlocked the door to her room. "Welcome," she said.

A cherrywood daybed was positioned against the wall and a small round table, also made of cherry, and two chairs were just off the compact kitchen. The apartment was meticulously kept. The bed was made and there were no dirty dishes in the sink, or clean ones in the rack. A dainty teapot with a cozy covering it was the only object on the counter.

"The vases are in the top cupboard over the sink. Would you be so kind as to get them?" Ruth asked. "You'll need to stand on a chair."

"On one of those chairs?" Charlotte asked. They were too nice to stand on.

"If you don't mind."

Charlotte slipped off her shoes, positioned a chair in front of the sink, and climbed onto it. As soon as she opened the cupboard she wanted to close it. She'd stumbled on a treasure chest. She was afraid to touch the vases, let alone remove them from the cupboard. They were crystal—antique crystal, she was sure.

"Ruth, these are beautiful." Charlotte turned her eyes down toward the older woman.

"Yes, indeed, they are, and very underused. Your flowers came in the nick of time."

Charlotte carefully picked up a vase and stepped down from the chair, placing the beautiful piece of crystal on the counter. She repeated the process five times. "There," she said, closing the cupboard. "Would you like me to help arrange the flowers?"

"Oh no, deary. The pleasure is all mine. But do you mind leaving your bucket? Could you pick it up tomorrow?"

Charlotte hadn't planned to come into town tomorrow, but she told Ruth it wouldn't be a problem. It would be nice to see what the woman did with the flowers.

Ruth opened the top drawer beside the sink. As Charlotte replaced the chair, Ruth put on an apron and then carefully rolled up the sleeves of her white blouse. "In fact," Ruth said, "you might consider asking Stephanie if you can help her tomorrow. She has a tea planned for all of us ladies, but I'm afraid she's doing too much. She says she has a month until the baby comes, but I'm afraid she's mistaken." Ruth clucked her tongue. "She could use an experienced hand."

Charlotte smiled and patted Ruth's hand. "I'll talk to Stephanie on the way out. I'll see you tomorrow."

Charlotte stopped for a second in the hall. Why had she been so ready to say yes to Ruth? It was almost as if the woman held some sort of control over her. She headed down the hall to the lobby and stopped to look for Stephanie.

A voice from above startled her. It was Red, his head poking over the railing. "The little lady went that way," he said, pointing down the hall.

Charlotte waved up at him and called out thanks. It was already nine fifteen. She was tempted to head home. Surely Stephanie didn't really need her help tomorrow.

But she turned the hall just as Stephanie came out of the restroom. The young woman started to say something, but stopped. She put her arm out, leaned her hand against the wall, and began blowing through her mouth.

"Are you okay?" Charlotte asked.

Stephanie shook her head. "Go get Ruth," she managed to say. "And hurry."

Chapter Two

It wasn't until Charlotte was running up the stairs, taking them two at a time, that she wondered why Stephanie hadn't asked her to get the RN on duty from the nursing-home side of the care facility, but by then she was on the landing of the second floor, hurrying past Red.

"Is everything on the up and up?" he asked, still leaning against the rail.

Charlotte nodded and kept speed walking, second-guessing herself at leaving Stephanie in the hallway by herself. She knocked on Ruth's door.

"Coming!"

It seemed like hours until the door swung open and Charlotte could blurt out Stephanie's request.

Ruth didn't say a thing except, "Come on." She marched past Red and practically flew down the stairs, charging forward.

"Stephanie," she called out, turning into the hall. "I'm here."

Stephanie had her back against the wall. "I think the baby's coming," she said.

"Can you walk?" Ruth asked.

Stephanie shook her head.

"Charlotte, can you drive us across the street to the medical center?"

Charlotte held up her keys. "Of course."

"Or we can call for the ambulance," Ruth said. "What do you need, Stephanie?"

"A ride."

Ruth took Stephanie's elbow, and they began walking toward the lobby. Charlotte hurried ahead to open the door.

"Red," Ruth called out. "Please find Nurse Louise and ask her to telephone the clinic and tell them we're on our way."

Red saluted from the mezzanine.

"Thank you," Stephanie muttered as she waddled through the open door.

IN THE CAR, Stephanie called her husband on her cell phone and left a message. "He's in Grand Island, interviewing for a job," she said.

Charlotte stared straight ahead as she pulled onto the street. Chances were, he wouldn't make it in time. As she pulled into the clinic parking lot, Stephanie gasped. "It really hurts," she squealed.

"Yes, dear, it's supposed to feel that way," Ruth said calmly. "Take a deep breath."

Charlotte parked the car and slammed it into park, turning off the ignition. "I'll go tell them we're here."

She rushed through the automatic doors. "There's a

woman in the parking lot ready to have a baby," Charlotte called out to the receptionist.

She raced back to the parking lot. The back door of the car was open and Ruth stood on the pavement, leaning into the car. A young man pushing a wheelchair appeared.

"Can we get her out of the car?" Charlotte asked.

"I think so." Ruth leaned forward. "Come on, Stephie, let's get you into the hospital."

Stephanie began scooting toward the door.

"I think she's doing fine," Ruth whispered to Charlotte. "There's no reason to be alarmed." Ruth took one arm and Charlotte took the other and guided her to the wheelchair. "Another contraction is starting," she gasped.

"That means they're about three minutes apart, dear. We'll know soon how you're progressing," Ruth said, marching ahead, leading the way.

"I was going to have the baby in Harding." Stephanie grasped the armrests of the chair as the orderly pushed.

"We'll see, deary," Ruth said, "after Dr. Carr takes a look."

Charlotte walked alongside, wanting to take Stephanie's hand, to take some of her pain. Her eyes filled with tears. Thoughts of Denise having her babies filled her head. Charlotte hadn't been with her when Sam, Emily, and Christopher were born. Each time, Denise had called hours after the baby arrived. Each time, Charlotte wished her daughter had called before so she could have been praying for her while she labored. Charlotte offered up a prayer now, for Stephanie's safety and the baby's too, as they all pushed through the double doors of the clinic.

The aide wheeled Stephanie into the first room. "I'll go

see how much longer Dr. Carr will be." The young man looked nervous, as if they might expect him to deliver the baby.

"Let's get you on the bed," Ruth said, helping Stephanie stand. Ruth deftly lowered the bar along the bed and helped Stephanie get situated. "Try rolling onto your side," she suggested. "That's often more comfortable." Another contraction gripped Stephanie and Ruth massaged the small of her back.

Charlotte hurried out the door as she marveled at Ruth's calmness and the fact that the old woman seemed to know what she was doing. As she approached the receptionist, the woman said that Dr. Carr was just finishing up with a patient.

"What about the nurse on duty?"

"She's helping him—with sutures," the receptionist said.

Charlotte took a deep breath. "Doesn't the baby take precedence?"

"They'll be here soon," the receptionist said.

Charlotte walked back to Stephanie's room, thinking maybe the young woman wasn't as close to delivering as it seemed. After all, it was a first baby, and everyone knew they could take days. Charlotte had been in labor with Bill for thirty-six hours. She knocked on the door.

"Come in, please," Ruth's strong voice called out.

A contraction was just ending and Ruth was wiping Stephanie's forehead. The young woman propped herself up on her elbow. "Could you hand me my purse, please? I want to try my husband again."

Just as Stephanie started to dial, her cell phone rang. It

was her husband. "He's on his way," Stephanie said, collapsing back down on the bed as Dr. Carr came into the room.

"Well, well, well," he said. He chatted with Stephanie for a minute and then said he needed to take a look to see whether she could make it to Harding or if she should stay in Bedford.

Charlotte slipped out into the hall, and a few minutes later Ruth came out. "She's nine centimeters dilated," she said. "She's staying here."

"Do you think her husband will make it?" Charlotte asked.

Ruth looked skeptical. "She's advancing quickly for a first birth—although it sounds like she's been in labor since last night and just didn't realize it."

"Do you want a ride home?"

"Oh, no. I'm going to stay here and support Stephanie."

"Then I'll stay and support you," Charlotte said.

"Oh, that's not necessary." Ruth put her hand against the wall as if to steady herself.

"No, I insist. I'll wait out here in the hall."

Ruth smiled. "That's awfully kind of you." She sighed. "I do wish I had a camera."

Charlotte pulled hers out of her purse. "Look. Use mine."

The older woman smiled again and took the camera. "I can't thank you enough. It was providential that you stopped by today."

AN HOUR LATER, Dr. Carr, the nurse, and Ruth were with Stephanie when a young man with sandy hair and freckles hurried through the door of the clinic. The receptionist pointed to the first room and Charlotte stood up from her chair in the hall, ceasing her prayers for a moment, and pointed to the door.

He stopped beside Charlotte. "Can I just go inside?"

"Are you Stephanie's husband?"

He nodded.

"Then get in there!"

As the young man pushed through the door, Stephanie let out a yelp that sounded full of both pain and relief.

Fifteen minutes later Ruth came out of the room, the camera in her hand. "It's a girl," she said.

Charlotte hugged the woman and then guided her down onto the chair.

"My, my," Ruth said. "I'm definitely too old for this. Thank goodness for Dr. Carr—and that it was a quick delivery."

It hadn't seemed quick. "And everything is all right?" Charlotte asked.

"Perfect," Ruth said, pushing her silver hair away from her face. "You know, I never thought I'd see another birth. I can't tell you what a blessing it is." The old woman closed her eyes and leaned her head against the wall.

"Ruth?" Charlotte asked.

"I'm fine, deary. Just tired."

THE LOBBY OF BEDFORD GARDENS was full of residents when Charlotte and Ruth arrived. "I'll go check with the kitchen and get you some lunch," Charlotte said to the older woman.

"No, no." Red stepped forward. "I already ordered a sandwich for her. I'll go get it."

Ruth collapsed into a chair, and several of the other residents flocked around her, asking how Stephanie was.

"Remarkable," Ruth said. "I've never had a patient who did as well, not in all my years as a nurse." She told them that the baby weighed in at six pounds. And although she was four weeks early, her lungs were strong.

Red returned with the sandwich, and after he handed it to Ruth, he bent and kissed her cheek. "Attagirl," Red said, as Ruth blushed. "You saved the day."

"She'd been in labor since last night and didn't realize it," Ruth said. "Poor thing."

"And you're sure the baby is going to be okay?" a woman with hair like cotton balls who sat in a wheelchair said softly, nearly a whisper.

"I'm certain of it, Aggie." Ruth sank deeper into the chair.

"And what did Stephanie name her?" a woman with long gray hair asked.

"She and her husband are still deciding," Ruth said. "But I think they may be leaning toward the name Lillian." Ruth winked at Charlotte and then took a bite of her sandwich. Charlotte smiled. Stephanie had wanted to name the baby Ruth, but the older woman had forbidden it and suggested Lillian, thinking about the lilies that Charlotte had brought in.

"Let Ruthie eat her lunch," Red said. "We'll be able to talk with her later." He made a shooing motion and the other residents began to disperse, but he pulled a chair closer to Ruth's and sat down. Charlotte did too.

"Eat half of this, deary." Ruth extended the plate. "It's way too much for me."

Famished, Charlotte took the sandwich.

"Who will be our activities coordinator now?" Red asked, rubbing the top of his shiny head.

Ruth shrugged. "That will work itself out. I'm sure the director has a plan." Then she turned her head toward Charlotte. "We're going to need your help tomorrow though for the tea. I know exactly what needs to be done, but I can't do it all."

Charlotte finished the last bite of the sandwich. "What time?" Charlotte asked. It wouldn't hurt to wait another day to make her list of catch-up chores to do around the house and farm.

"Come at twelve thirty. The tea is scheduled for two o'clock."

"It will be my pleasure."

"You should get on home now," Ruth said.

Charlotte stood. "After I help you to your room and arrange the bouquets while you rest."

"I can help with that," Red said.

"Well, well." Ruth placed the sandwich plate on the table and struggled to her feet. "Many hands make light work. Both of you, come along. We'll be done in no time."

BY THE TIME CHARLOTTE LEFT the nursing home it was three fifteen. She'd called Bob from Ruth's apartment and left a message on the home phone. Surely, if he got worried about her, he would check the voice mail, wouldn't he? She actually wasn't sure if he remembered how to check the messages, even though Emily had shown him.

The kids would be home from school in no time. Had she finished the dishes before she left the house with Christopher? She yawned, suddenly tired after all the excitement. Her adrenaline rush was coming to an end.

She slowed by the school. The students were pouring onto the bus. She searched the parking lot for Sam's car but didn't see it. She didn't see Christopher on the bus either—perhaps he'd caught a ride with Sam.

Charlotte stopped at the pharmacy and dropped off the film, and then hurried on toward Heather Creek Farm. She couldn't remember, in all her days, having such an exciting first day of school. There was nothing like the birth of a baby. In a split second, Charlotte was thinking about Denise again. Had Kevin been a big help after the babies were born? Did she have friends who brought meals? Charlotte's heart skipped a beat. Oh, how she wished she had been able to go out and help. Charlotte held on to the steering wheel with her right hand and ran her left hand through her short hair, and then turned onto Heather Creek Road. A minute later Toby rushed out to greet her and then turned to run, panting as she did, alongside the car as if she were herding Charlotte toward the house. It wasn't often that Charlotte was gone from the farm all day.

She rounded the corner of the driveway. Sam's car was parked by the house but none of the kids were outside. She hurried into the house, ready to tell them about her day and ask about theirs.

As she closed the back door, Christopher called out, "Grandma's home!"

"Oh," Emily replied from the family room, and then she yelled, "Grandma's home!"

"Is there an echo in the house?" Charlotte asked as she put her purse on the dining room table.

"No," Christopher answered, a little too loudly.

"How was your first day of sixth grade?" Charlotte asked him.

"Good."

Emily stepped into the kitchen.

"And how was your day?" Charlotte asked.

"Great."

Charlotte peeked into the family room. "Where's Sam?"

Christopher shot Emily a look just as Charlotte heard Sam's voice on the staircase. Then she heard another voice, a female voice.

"Sam?" Charlotte called out as she headed down the hall to the entryway. On the staircase stood Sam and Arielle, a frown spread across his face and a smile frozen on hers.

"I was giving Arielle a tour of the house," Sam finally said. "That's all."

Chapter Three

Sam grabbed a chocolate chip cookie from the plate that Emily plopped down in the middle of the table and then remembered his manners. He passed the plate to Arielle. "How about a glass of milk too?" he asked.

"Please," she answered. Her usually smiling face and bright blue eyes were somber. It wasn't like they'd been doing anything wrong. She'd said how much she liked the house, and he had offered to give her a tour. He hadn't even shown her his room—it was too messy. He'd used the excuse that Grandma wouldn't approve. When he tried to tell Grandma that, she'd just given him the old stinky eye followed by a thick layer of guilt. Why did Grandma always have to overreact?

"Don't worry about it," Emily said.

Grandma had gone down the hall after lecturing Sam about not having guests over when she wasn't home. And then she told them she'd been at the nursing home and then the clinic all day and something about a baby being born. How was he supposed to know that? He'd expected her to be home.

"It's not a big deal, really." Emily said to Arielle. "Grandma's not upset—she just wanted to make sure Sam understood the rules." Emily shot one of her sassy looks across the table.

He sat up straight and smiled at Arielle. He didn't want her to feel bad. Today had been a great start to the school year. He had senior English, sociology, physics, yearbook, and study hall with Arielle. What could be better? He'd hurried to each class, determined to get there first, to see if she would choose a seat next to him. Each time she did, passing up sitting by her friends. She chose him every time.

Emily was right. He couldn't let the stuff with Grandma ruin his, or Arielle's, day. He stood and strutted across the kitchen to the fridge for the pitcher of milk. He filled two glasses and placed them on the table, one in front of Arielle and one at his place.

"Hey," Emily said. "What about me?"

"Hey," he said, intending to say, *What about you?* But then he looked at Arielle smiling up at him. "Hey," Sam said, nodding at the glass of milk. "You can have this one." He scooted the glass kitty-corner across the table to his sister and headed back to the fridge. "Do you want a glass of milk too?" he asked Christopher, who had just banged through the back door. He'd probably snuck outside to avoid the conflict between Sam and Grandma. That was something the kid hated.

"Are you feeling okay?" his little brother asked, kicking off his shoes.

Sam ignored him and pulled two more glasses from the cupboard. That was the thing about Arielle; she really did bring out the best in him.

His hand bumped against the cold coffeepot as he

poured the milk. Grandma seemed really tired. Maybe she'd like some coffee. That would impress Arielle; it was kind of like turning the other cheek, or loving your enemies. That stuff they talked about at youth group. He began opening cupboards. Where did she keep the stuff? There it was, right above the coffeepot. He opened the can and pulled out a scoop and began to tinker with the pot.

"You need a filter," Emily said. "It goes in the top."

He found the filter in the same cupboard and placed it in the machine and then filled the pot with water.

"It goes in the back." Emily was standing beside him. "And it's three scoops of coffee."

"I got it," he said, waving her away. He measured out three scoops and dumped it in the filter. Then added another half scoop, just to make sure. Grandma always said she liked her coffee strong. He flipped the switch with a flourish and slapped his hands together.

As the coffee started to brew, filling the kitchen with that homey scent, Sam sat down at the table and ate his cookie. Grandma headed into the kitchen from the hallway. "Emily!" Grandma exclaimed. "You started coffee for me."

Sam felt all warm inside.

"Actually, it was Sam." Emily shot him another funny look.

"Thank you," Grandma said, a confused look on her face. "That's just what I needed."

Christopher started talking about school, and his new teacher, who was only an inch taller than he was. "I'll have her beat in another month," he said proudly. Before Sam could think of something to say to Arielle, Christopher was off talking about the school newspaper. "Both the fifth and sixth graders can write for it," he explained, tipping back his chair until Grandma snapped her fingers. Christopher landed it back in place with a thud. "Last year it was all girls who were the reporters, so the articles were all about birthday parties and kittens. Stuff like that."

"What are you thinking, Christopher?" Grandma asked, sitting at the opposite end of the table with her coffee, right between Sam and Arielle.

"That I'm going to write articles about other stuff."

"Such as?" Grandma wrapped her hands around her coffee cup. Sam didn't understand how she could drink that stuff when it was so hot out. The thermometer by the shed read 102 degrees. Pretty hot for the first day of school.

Christopher shrugged. "We'll see."

Grandma asked Arielle if she was going to work during the school year.

She seemed to relax. "Yep, I found a new job, at Kepler's Pharmacy."

"That's great!" Grandma looked at Sam as she said it. He knew what she was thinking, but Sam was still trying to figure out how he would have time to keep his part-time job at the airport.

"Yeah, I'm really thankful for it. I need to save money."

Sam nearly groaned. Instead he grabbed another cookie, determined not to make eye contact with Grandma.

"I start at the pharmacy tomorrow," Arielle added, turning her glass of milk around and around. "Every dime is going into my college account."

Sam took a bite of his cookie. He knew what was coming next. Grandma was going to say something to him about college. But she didn't. Instead she asked Arielle where she planned to go.

"Harding State, probably. Then maybe I'll transfer to the University of Nebraska. Right now I'm thinking about becoming a nurse."

Grandma smiled and didn't even look toward Sam.

He took a bite of the cookie, relieved.

"What do you plan to study, Sam?" Arielle asked.

He sputtered and then swallowed wrong and started to cough. After a drink of milk, he said, "Oh, right now I'm just working on a plan for a new set of wheels for my car."

Arielle's mouth turned down just a little. Was that a frown? Now Grandma was frowning at him too.

Sam stuffed the rest of his cookie in his mouth. "Want to go check out the horses?" he asked, spitting out crumbs.

"Sure," Arielle said and then lifted the glass of milk to her mouth.

EMILY AND CHRISTOPHER tagged along, but soon the girls fell behind Sam. He turned around to hurry them up. Emily was smaller than Arielle and her hair was longer. Arielle's black hair bounced on her shoulders as she walked and her arms swung back and forth. He liked that about her. She seemed determined.

"Come on," Sam said. "Let's go down to the corral."

Christopher groaned. "Since when do you like the horses?"

Sam ignored him. It was hotter than hot. The girls were taking their time, and he and Christopher waited at the fence for them. He thought seeing the horses would impress Arielle, but he didn't want to go into the corral without Emily. Britney didn't seem very fond of him, and he was afraid he'd make a fool of himself if he tried to show off.

"Pete must have been working with Britney this afternoon," Emily said, climbing over the fence. Sam and Arielle followed her lead. Christopher climbed halfway up the fence and stayed there.

Britney trotted toward Emily and she greeted the horse with affection.

"Do you like to ride?" Arielle asked Sam.

"So-so," Sam said, wondering what Arielle wanted him to say. Would she like him more if he were into horses?

Christopher snickered from his perch on the other side of the fence.

"Emily said I could come out and ride with you on Saturday."

"Don't you have to work?"

"Not until noon." Arielle turned around, watching Emily with Britney. "Emily said that Britney belonged to your mom."

Sam nodded. He hadn't talked about Mom to Arielle and didn't want to now, not in the corral, not with Christopher listening. Honestly, he didn't want to talk about Mom at all.

"That's really cool," Arielle said. Her eyes were so kind. She tucked a strand of hair behind her ear. "So where will we ride on Saturday?"

"Maybe along the creek," Sam answered. He had no idea where Emily usually rode.

"That would be so cool."

AFTER DINNER, as Sam loaded the dishwasher, Emily bumped against him, opened the cabinet door under the sink, and grabbed the kitchen scrap bucket. "Want me to show you how to ride tonight?" she asked.

"Nah," Sam said. "I'm good."

"How can you be good? You never ride."

He ignored her.

She swung the bucket back and forth as she headed for the back door. "You should at least come out and learn how to saddle one of the horses—before you make a fool of yourself on Saturday."

"Maybe," he said, squirting soap into the little box in the dishwasher.

Sam stood at the kitchen window and watched Emily head out to the chicken coop. Finding out how to put a saddle on might not be that bad of an idea. That way he could help Arielle with hers. A minute later, Sam stood in the doorway to the family room. Grandpa dozed in his chair and Grandma sat in her rocking chair, a piece of embroidery in her hand.

"I'm going to go help Emily with the horses," he said.

Grandma squinted at him. "How come?"

"Well," Sam said, and then paused. "Well," he said again. "Emily invited Arielle to ride."

"And you plan to ride with them?" Grandma placed the embroidery in her lap.

Sam nodded. "On Saturday."

Grandma raised her eyebrows. "Okay."

Sam lumbered out the door and headed toward the chicken coop. He'd help Emily with the horses, feed them maybe, but he wasn't going on a ride tonight. Saturday would be fine. How hard could it be?

Chapter Four

Charlotte stood in the lobby of Bedford Gardens amazed at the transformation. Seven round tables covered with linen cloths were arranged around the room. Bouquets of lilies, the ones she had brought the day before, were arranged in Ruth's crystal vases and graced the tables, which were set with dainty china and real silver.

"Hello, dear." Ruth stood on the staircase, two teapots in her hands. "You're just in time." She wore a lacy white blouse and a pleated pink skirt. "I'm just about ready to get started on the food."

"Who helped you with all of this?"

"Red set up the tables and chairs. And Connie, one of the aides, carried down my boxes of china." Ruth carefully stepped down from the last stair and placed the teapots on two of the tables. "I just have the last two teapots to bring down."

"I'll do that," Charlotte said.

At the top of the stairs, she almost bumped into Red. He carried a stack of cloth napkins. "Oh, I'm glad to see you," he said, his eyes twinkling. "I'm afraid Ruth is going to wear herself out." He chuckled. "And me too."

"Is anyone else helping?" Charlotte moved away from the handrail, hoping that Red would take it.

"The aides, of course. It was Stephanie's idea, really—a birthday tea for Ruth. Who deserves it more? But then with the baby coming and all we probably should have just canceled it." Red started down the stairs.

"Wait. It's Ruth's birthday?"

Red nodded. "Today's the day."

Would it be rude to ask how old she is?

"And you'd never guess her age." His eyes twinkled again.

Charlotte shook her head. "I wouldn't dare try."

"No, and you shouldn't. I'll give you a hint." He leaned toward Charlotte. "I'm eighty-five." And then he whispered. "And she was—I still can't believe this—ten when I was born."

"No," Charlotte said. How could Ruth be ninety-five? Not that spunky woman who had so deftly handled the crisis the day before.

Red nodded, clearly pleased with himself. "Unbelievable, isn't it?"

Charlotte agreed as she wondered what Ruth and Red's relationship was, exactly. Ruth seemed to rely on Red and he seemed awfully fond of her. She smiled and then suddenly missed Bob. He hadn't come in for lunch by the time she left, and she had put sandwiches and soup in the fridge with a note. They'd hardly had a chance to chat last night, but tomorrow that would all change. They'd soon be back to their normal routine.

AT TWO O'CLOCK SHARP the ladies of Bedford Gardens gathered in the lobby to celebrate Ruth's birthday. Ruth stood at the head table, beaming, her cheeks rosy. Her head was adorned with a hat that would have made the queen mother proud—it was white and wide-brimmed with a rose-colored silk peony on the front. "Welcome, welcome," Ruth said. "And many thanks to each of you for celebrating the beginning of my ninety-sixth year on this good earth with me."

She continued, "As we enjoy each other's company, I want to remember our sweet Stephanie and her baby." She smiled broadly and then continued, "And I want to thank Charlotte Stevenson for the beautiful flowers and for joining us today." Ruth extended her arm toward Charlotte, who stood in the back of the lobby wearing the second of Ruth's aprons. Charlotte nodded as the women applauded. "I so hope," Ruth said, folding her hands together, "that you will join us often, Charlotte."

As Charlotte and Connie served the women the cucumber and cream cheese sandwiches and the cookies and little cakes that Stephanie had ordered from Mel's Place, a short older man, about Charlotte's age, in a nice suit approached her. "I'm Oscar Smith," he said. He had a full head of gray hair and wore a big class ring on his right hand.

"Pleased to meet you," Charlotte said as she shook his hand, balancing two plates of sandwiches in her left hand.

"I manage this facility and one in Harding," the man said.

Charlotte nodded. He was also the owner, if she remembered the story in the *Bedford Leader* a couple of months ago correctly.

"I just stopped by to see Stephanie at your little clinic," he said. "I'm afraid her having the baby so early caught me off guard. I haven't hired anyone to replace her."

Charlotte smiled. What did this have to do with her?

"Could we chat for a moment?" Oscar asked. "In my office."

"Sure," Charlotte said, placing the plates on the tables beside her.

"I'll be right back," she said to Connie and followed Oscar down the hall. If Oscar Smith wanted to thank her for helping out yesterday and today, he could just say so. He didn't need to be so formal. He held the door open to his office and Charlotte walked through.

"Go ahead and sit down," Oscar said, closing the door and motioning to the wingback chair closest to the wall. He sat in the matching chair, closest to the door.

As he settled into his chair, he said, "Both Stephanie and the nurse . . ." He paused as if he couldn't remember the name. "Louise, right?"

Charlotte nodded.

He continued. "Both told me what a big help you were yesterday and here you are again today too. I really appreciate it." He drummed his fingers on the desk. "Have you been volunteering here long?"

Charlotte told him about the request at church to serve the residents and how she came in with flowers—it felt like over a month ago, not just yesterday—and how Ruth had asked her to come back today. "I really haven't volunteered at all," she said, "except for today."

"Well, no matter," he said as he leaned forward. "Would

you be willing to work with us for a short while? Just until I can fill Stephanie's position."

"Pardon?" What exactly was he asking?

He repeated what he'd just said, verbatim.

"Are you offering me a job, Mr. Smith?" It had been years since anyone had offered her a job—besides making pies.

"A part-time, very temporary job," he answered.

"How many hours a week?"

"Ten? Fifteen?" he was questioning her.

Ten hours a week—that would be just two hours a day. "And what exactly would my duties be?"

"To organize and execute an activity each afternoon. A game. A craft. A tea."

"And what makes you think I'm qualified?" Charlotte asked.

"I've asked around." He folded his large hands together. "Actually, I stopped for coffee at Mel's Place and asked if anyone there knew you. Your recommendations are glowing." His eyes twinkled as he spoke.

Charlotte winced. Her sweet friend Melody hardly qualified as objective. Still she was flattered and almost said yes on the spot. Then she remembered the kids. And the farm. And Bob. And all the tasks she needed to complete, all the things she needed to put on her to-do list. "Let me talk to my husband when I get home," she said. "I'll give you a call and let you know."

He handed her a card and shook her hand again. "It really would be a big help."

A minute later Charlotte stood in the back of the lobby and scanned the tables, her heart racing. *A job!* At her age. Suddenly she felt years younger.

Connie held up a teapot. "Could you fill this?" she called out to Charlotte.

She took the teapot and headed back to the kitchen. She couldn't see how working a couple of hours a day would make things any more stressful at home. She would just need to be organized. And, after yesterday's surprise of finding Sam and Arielle in the house unsupervised, she'd need to make sure and get home before the children did. She filled the teapot and hurried back into the lobby. Each of the tables had a platter of sandwiches, a bowl of cantaloupe and watermelon balls, a plate of cookies, and a full pot of tea now. Connie was moving among the women, pouring tea, passing platters, and visiting. It was clear that she enjoyed her work and was good at it.

The women residents, who all wore summer dresses and old-fashioned hats, chatted as they sipped their tea and took bites of food. Most of them weren't exactly dainty because their hands shook a little, and many of them nearly shouted as they visited. But they were all beautiful.

As Charlotte served sandwiches and cookies to the ladies and then snuck some goodies up the stairs to Red, who sat at his usual place on the mezzanine, she thought about Mr. Smith's offer. It would be a wonderful, fulfilling place to work, and it was only temporary, after all. She slowed as she came back down the stairs. That actually made her a little sad. Maybe she could apply for the permanent position, if Mr. Smith kept it very part time. Could she do that once the soybean harvest started? Sometimes Bob and Pete needed her to drive truck or run into town for parts. Well, there was no reason to think about that now. In the meantime, even the money from a temporary job would help;

she could put it toward Sam's college fund, a fund that at the moment didn't exist.

A couple of the women mentioned that it was naptime as Charlotte headed into the kitchen with a stack of dirty plates and began loading the dishwasher.

"Thank you so much, deary." Ruth placed a stack of dishes on the counter. "What did Mr. Smith ask you about?"

"About filling in for Stephanie temporarily."

"Oh, that would be lovely." Ruth's eyes danced as she spoke. Charlotte continued loading the dishwasher and a couple of minutes later Ruth returned with a second load, but as she placed the plates on the counter she stumbled.

"Oh, Ruth," Charlotte said, reaching out to steady her. "You shouldn't be doing this."

"I'm fine," Ruth said. "Just a little short of breath. I'll sit for a minute." She walked slowly to a chair in the corner of the kitchen and sat down.

"How about a glass of water?" Charlotte ran the cold tap and retrieved a clean glass from the cupboard. "Here you—"

"Deary," Ruth interrupted. "Would you be so kind as to ask Red to get my nitroglycerin? It's in the cabinet in my bath."

Charlotte started to ask Ruth if she was okay, but of course she wasn't; she wouldn't be asking for her nitro if she were. "Ruth—" Charlotte took a step forward. The older woman had turned a sickly white and had begun to slump against the wall.

"Help!" Charlotte called out, rushing forward, sloshing water on the floor as she wrapped her arm around Ruth.

"What is it?" Aggie, the woman in the wheelchair, sat in

the doorway with a teapot in her lap. A spry woman named Betty was right behind her.

"Call 911. Get the nurse! Tell Red to get Ruth's nitro."

Betty turned around in a hurry. "Red!" she yelled. "Red!"

Aggie spun around in her wheelchair, the teapot still in her lap. "I'll get the nurse," she said softly just as Connie hurried into the kitchen. Before Charlotte could say anything, Connie was speaking into a device she'd pulled from her belt, asking for help immediately in the kitchen.

Charlotte looked into Ruth's face.

"So sorry, deary," Ruth whispered. "Don't be too alarmed. This gets the better of me every once in a while, I'm afraid."

Chapter Five

Emily walked beside Ashley down the hall of Bedford High toward their lockers, both carrying their sketch pads. Art class rocked this year, all because of the new teacher, Ms. Carey. She'd worked as a jewelry designer in Chicago before going back to school to become an art teacher, and she seemed to know about fashion design too, about clothes and all that. She'd mentioned some of the TV shows that highlighted new designers and how much fun it was to watch and critique the work along with the judges. Unlike most adults, she actually seemed to think that one could earn a living doing something artistic.

"Do you work today?" Emily asked Ashley.

As Ashley nodded, her auburn curls bounced on her shoulders. "Mom needs me right away. She needs to buy supplies in Harding today."

Ashley was so lucky to have a mom who owned a café. It was the perfect job for a teenage girl. Emily closed her locker and turned around, ready to head out to the parking lot, as Arielle called out a hello. She held her pharmacy smock in her hand. Emily looked around for Sam but didn't see him. "Is Sam giving you a ride?" she asked.

Arielle shifted her books to her other hand. "No, he's talking with Mr. Anderson." The sociology teacher. Was Sam in trouble already? It was only the second day of school. Emily really wanted to go by the pharmacy and buy the latest *Vogue*.

Emily said good-bye to Ashley and Arielle, and the two headed out the front doors together.

Emily ambled down the hall. No reason to hurry if Sam was being interrogated. It might take awhile. As she neared the office, Ms. Carey nearly assaulted her with the door. She stopped, a cup of coffee in her hand. "Emily!" she said. "I didn't mean to almost run you over."

"No problem." Emily smiled.

"I meant to tell you how much I like your skirt," Ms. Carey said.

Emily glanced down. She was wearing the brown and pink outfit she'd bought in Harding the week before, with brown flip-flops. The skirt was short and the top barely passed Grandma's requirements. "Thank you," she said, looking up.

"Did you make it?"

Emily shook her head.

"Do you sew?" Ms. Carey stood by the trophy cabinet.

"A little." Emily was aware of their reflections in the cabinet.

"Have you ever made your own pattern?"

"One time. For a fundraiser." It had been for the prom dress for the sewing contest. She smiled, expecting

Ms. Carey to ask her more about it, but just then Mr. Santos, the counselor, approached and Ms. Carey smiled at Emily. "See you tomorrow."

Emily walked toward the front doors. She thought it had been hot in the building until she hit the outdoors. She could feel the heat of the concrete step through the plastic of her flip-flops. Arielle was walking quickly toward downtown. Just ahead of her, Ashley was headed to Mel's Place. That was what Emily needed—a job, something Grandma would approve of, something that wouldn't interfere with her schoolwork. Emily frowned. She wasn't sure what that would be. She would like to learn more about design, but she knew how expensive fabric and notions were. Too bad Aunt Rosemary wouldn't hire her to work at Fabrics and Fun on Saturdays, but Grandma told her that the store barely made enough money for her great aunt to support herself, let alone pay someone else.

She watched as students climbed into their cars and drove away and the buses pulled away from the curb. Christopher waved at her from the back of one of them. The little stinker—she thought he was riding home with them. He probably got tired of waiting, and at this rate he would beat them home.

A minute later, Sam ran down the stairs. "Is everyone gone?" he asked.

Emily stood. "It depends on who you mean by everyone."

"You know," he said.

"Arielle?"

He nodded.

"She walked to work."

"I was going to give her a ride." Sam started for the parking lot. "But Mr. Anderson wanted to clarify something he'd said in class, like I really cared."

"Hey, I need to go to the pharmacy." Emily hurried to keep up with her brother.

"Why?"

"To get a fashion magazine."

Sam opened the door to his car. "You'll have to hide it from Grandma—she hates that stuff."

"No she doesn't." Emily climbed into the passenger seat. Actually Grandma did, but maybe she wouldn't if Emily were only interested in the designs, not how everyone looked and the stories that Grandma claimed were, at the very least, questionable. And Grandma said all of the models were skinny and undernourished. Emily fastened her seat belt. "Besides, it's for an art project at school." At least she hoped it would be soon. "A design assignment." She did need to make a collage. She could use the pictures for that, if nothing else.

Sam looked at her as if he didn't believe her, but it didn't really matter, because he was already headed toward Kepler's Pharmacy.

EMILY THUMBED THROUGH an *Elle* magazine, stopping at a spread on fall plaids. The models wore clunky, retro platform shoes. She flipped to a spread on winter peacoats, blue and black and gray. She'd seen some on Forever 21's Web site for twenty bucks. The ones in the magazine were $260. She put *Elle* back in its slot and pulled out *Vogue*.

In the next aisle several guys wearing matching shorts and jerseys walked by, guys she didn't recognize. One of them was exceptionally tall. She stepped away from the magazine rack and scanned the pharmacy.

"Hey," the tall guy said, facing the checkout stand. "Where's your Icy Hot?" HARDING STATE was inscribed across the back of his jersey.

"Um, I think that's aisle three," Arielle answered.

Emily held on to the magazine and walked toward the checkout. Three of the guys stood in line with snacks and Vitamin Waters in their hands as Arielle checked out a fourth player. A fifth stood to the side, a soccer ball in his hands. HARDING STATE COLLEGE MEN'S SOCCER was embroidered on his duffel bag. He wore his hair in a buzz cut; the start of a goatee looked like a smear of mud on his chin.

Sam stood by the door with his hands in his pockets and a smile on his face. "Where are you guys headed?" he asked number 8, who held the ball.

"Grand Island. We play tonight at eight."

"First game of the season?" Sam asked.

"It's a preseason game," number 8 answered. "We're playing Midwest Lutheran."

Sam nodded as if he knew what the guy was talking about. Emily rolled her eyes.

"Do you play?" The guy tossed the ball from one hand to the other.

"Nah."

Emily rolled her eyes again.

"Well, I used to," Sam said. "In California."

"Come on." Number 8 pushed open the door. "Let's kick the ball a little while those guys finish up in here."

Two of the other soccer players followed Sam and number 8 out the door as Arielle began ringing up the Icy Hot for the really tall player. Emily was pretty sure he was a goalie. She stood on her tiptoes, looking over the top of a sign in the window. Sam and number 8 were passing the ball back and forth on the sidewalk. Number 8 headed the ball and Sam dropped it to the sidewalk, trapping it. Pastor Nathan walked by as he tipped his baseball cap to Sam.

"Hey, Emily." Arielle was ready to ring up the magazine.

"Boy, you got a little busy, huh?" Emily placed the *Vogue* on the counter.

Arielle nodded. "I've never seen so many soccer players in my life. Sam must be in heaven."

Emily pointed out the window. "Yeah, he looks like he's having fun."

Arielle turned just as Sam dropped the ball from his chest to the sidewalk and then did a bicycle pass to the Icy Hot player. Obviously he was the goalie, because he whacked the ball hard, but Sam kicked it again, sending it past the goalie and down the sidewalk. The Harding players who had gathered around clapped as number 8 tore down the sidewalk after the soccer ball. Sam had a mixture of embarrassment and delight on his face. Arielle smiled as she turned back toward the register. "He's good, isn't he?"

Emily nodded, pulling out a ten-dollar bill—her allowance money—and handing it to Arielle. The magazine was expensive, but she was sure she'd find some good ideas.

Arielle handed Emily the *Vogue*, her change, and the receipt, and the two girls said good-bye.

As Emily stepped out onto the sidewalk she heard one of the players talking to Sam. "We have a new program going this year for high school players in Harding—those who aren't playing football."

Sunlight bounced off the team bus parked nearby and blinded Emily momentarily. She shielded her eyes as number 8 stepped forward, the soccer ball tucked under his arm, and joined the conversation with Sam. "Tryouts are next month. The date's on the Web site: September fifteenth, I think."

Sam shoved his hands in his pockets. "But I'm not from Harding."

"Doesn't matter," number 8 said. "It's club affiliated. It has nothing to do with schools."

"I'm pretty rusty," Sam said.

"You looked good to me," the guy with the Icy Hot said.

The last player came through the door, and number 8 tossed the ball in the air. "Let's go," he called out, catching the ball in his hands and jogging toward the bus.

Sam waved as the players filed onto the bus. Then he yelled, "Good luck in your game." Emily couldn't tell what he was thinking as he pushed back through the doors of the pharmacy to tell Arielle good-bye. She opened up the *Vogue* magazine and began thumbing through it as she headed down the sidewalk to Sam's 240-Z.

BACK AT HOME, Emily spread the *Vogue* open again as she sat at the computer and Googled one of the fashion-design shows. Why didn't they have cable? The show was on tomorrow night. All the girls at school talked about it.

She turned to a spread of illustrations in the magazine that looked like the old-fashioned patterns at Fabric and Fun. It would be really cool to do illustrations like that. They were definitely out of proportion, not drawn at all like how she was taught in art class.

The back door slammed shut. Emily glanced at the time on the computer: 8:20. It was growing dark outside. "Hey, my turn on the computer," Sam said before he'd even entered the room.

"Me first." Christopher ran into the room. "Before I have to go to bed." He looked like a wild horse had dragged him through the barnyard. The hair along his forehead was damp with sweat and pushed back, his shorts were torn at the hem, and he was filthy.

Grandma was right behind him. "Bath time, Christopher."

"I took one last night."

Grandma pointed at his arms and then his legs. "Christopher, you're covered with dirt."

"I was just running through the field, chasing Toby." He wiped his hands on his T-shirt, smearing more powdery dirt around.

"And throwing plums into the field." Grandma crossed her arms. "Don't think I didn't see you." She was trying not to look too serious. "Go straight upstairs," she said. "Don't touch anything."

Christopher let out a groan and turned on his heels. A second later the sound of his feet on the stairs reverberated through the family room.

"Come on, Emily." Sam tried to sit on the computer chair beside her, but she shifted her weight. "All you're doing is wasting time with that fashion stuff."

Grandma had started to the kitchen but stopped.

"And what? You're not going to be wasting time on Facebook?" Emily shot back.

"Actually . . ." Sam pushed against the chair. "I was going to look at colleges."

Grandma stepped back toward the computer. Emily could practically see her antennae shoot up.

"Yeah, right," Emily said. "That will be the day."

"Which college?" Grandma asked. Her voice didn't betray the anticipation that Emily was sure she felt.

"Harding State."

Emily closed down the fashion site. There was no way that Grandma would think fashion research took priority over colleges.

"Are you looking at a specific program?" Grandma took a step closer. Sam stood over her, but Emily still wasn't willing to relinquish the chair to him.

"Soccer," Emily said, spinning around in the chair. "That's what subject."

"It's still college," Sam said with a smirk.

"Please give Sam a turn," Grandma said.

Emily closed the window that she'd minimized and stood, glaring at Sam as he sat down.

"That would be great if you could play soccer at Harding State next year," Grandma said. "But first you need to do some work researching colleges—several of them."

Emily hugged the *Vogue* against her chest. "Not next year. This year. We saw the Harding State soccer team in town. They told him about a new club team for high school students."

"This year?" Grandma said. "I thought you wanted to look at the college. And how would you have time to do that and work at the airport?"

Sam groaned, sounding just like Christopher. "Next year is so far away. Besides, Ed Haffner basically said I can pick my hours at the airport, so I'm sure I could fit it all in."

"But you need to get started on researching college now, Sam. You have to plan ahead or it's not going to happen." Grandma's voice was sharp. "Did you make an appointment with Mr. Santos?"

"What are you talking about? School just started." Sam clicked onto the Web page describing the soccer program. "No one at school is talking about college yet."

"Then why does Arielle have an appointment with Mr. Santos tomorrow?" Emily plopped down on the couch as Sam scowled at her. "And look at me—I'm only a sophomore but I already have a plan. Parsons School of Design, New York City." She raised her hands over her head in victory.

"Please," Sam said. "Give it a break."

"Sam." Grandma sounded impatient. "It really is time to get serious."

He shrugged. "Take a look at this. Tryouts are September twelfth."

"Show me later," Grandma said. "I need to go talk to Grandpa about something before he falls asleep."

Grandma headed back into the kitchen.

"What's with Grandma?" Sam asked.

"She wants you to get an education." Emily smirked. "She wants you to be independent someday. She doesn't want you to live with her for the rest of your life."

"Not that. She's been acting funny. And she went back to the nursing home today." Sam spun around in the computer chair. "What's that all about?"

Emily shrugged. She never really thought about what Grandma did when they were in school; she just figured she did housework. Why would she want to go to the nursing home two days in a row? It had to be the most depressing place in town.

Chapter Six

Charlotte sat at the table staring into her morning coffee. Pete had done the milking and fed the horses, and Emily was finishing up the chickens. For the third morning in a row, all three kids had been up on time and on task. Was it just the first week of school? Or were they becoming responsible?

"Grandma," Christopher called out from the family room.

"What, sweetie?"

"I'm trying to figure out what to write about for the newspaper."

Charlotte rose from the table and walked into the family room, taking her coffee with her.

Christopher spun around in the computer chair. "I'm thinking about writing about manure."

"Manure?"

He nodded. "Did you know there's a manure pile in Monroe that burned for four months?"

"I had no idea."

"Yeah, isn't that wild?"

"But what does it have to do with your school? Or Bedford?" Charlotte put her hand on Christopher's shoulder.

"What do you mean?"

"Shouldn't your article be about something local? Not a sensational event in the next county over?"

"Oh." Christopher logged off the computer. "Still, it's interesting."

Charlotte sighed. Interesting was a matter of opinion, but it was very different from the stories about kittens and birthday parties that had inspired him to join the school newspaper staff. She padded back into the kitchen as Bob put his coffee cup in the sink. "I'm off," he said. "I'll see you at lunchtime."

"Hold on. What do you think if I help out at the nursing home?" Charlotte had told him about it last night, but then they hadn't had a chance to finish their conversation.

"Temporarily, right?"

Charlotte nodded as Emily, wearing a black miniskirt, a magenta top, and dangling earrings, hurried in through the back door, swinging a basket of eggs in her hand.

"And nothing's going to be different around here?" Bob grinned after he said it.

Charlotte frowned. "Well, I don't think—"

Emily interrupted her. "What's going to be different around here?"

Charlotte shook her head. "Grandpa and I were having a private conversation."

"Oh." Emily blushed a little and then yelled, "Christopher! We're leaving."

Bob kissed Charlotte on the cheek and then said, "Do what you think is best."

"What's best?" Emily asked, hurrying through the kitchen with her book bag.

"Emily." Charlotte shook her head again as Bob stepped out the back door. It was hard to have a conversation with Bob anymore, let alone finish one.

"Oh, right. Private. I remember." Emily slipped on her flats and tugged on her little black sweater. "Grandma, maybe you should go on a walk with Hannah. You know, if you're trying to figure something out."

Charlotte stood at the kitchen sink and watched the kids pile into Sam's car. What if she'd had a career all these years? Made money to contribute to the household? Set a good example for Denise? If she had, Charlotte might be working part-time now or retired with a pension.

Sam drove his 240-Z down the driveway, and Toby ran after the car, barking.

Emily was right. She needed to talk to Hannah.

"AND WHAT DO YOU WISH you had done all those years ago?" Hannah asked as they walked along Heather Creek.

Had she never shared this with Hannah? "Studied nursing."

"That's a great career," Hannah said, slapping at a mosquito. The pests were out early today. "So why not take the job at the nursing home? It sounds like a win-win situation."

Charlotte nodded. "But things seem a little intense there. I hope it won't become one of those situations where it starts to consume every spare minute of my time."

Hannah laughed. "Well, I'm sure someone doesn't go to the clinic every day, right?"

"I don't know." They turned onto the road that ran adjacent to Hannah and Frank's property. Charlotte took a dusty breath. Frank was plowing under the wheat stubble in the field across the road and had just turned the plow; the wind had twirled the soil into a dust devil. The two women were silent for a moment as they hurried down the lane.

Charlotte held her breath and then let it out and breathed in once they'd turned down by the creek. It was hard to describe what was bothering her. "There's a woman there—Ruth," she said, "who has reached out to me. Actually, she's reached out to everyone. But I think she's pretty ill. She's the one who went to the clinic yesterday; she has congestive heart disease."

"The one who helped Stephanie? When she was delivering her baby?"

Charlotte nodded. The dampness of the creek felt good, bringing a little bit of relief to the already warm morning.

"She sounds like a real spitfire," Hannah said.

Charlotte smiled. "She is, but in the nicest of ways."

"And you're worried she doesn't have long for this world?" Hannah asked.

"Something like that." Was that true? Was she afraid of spending time at Bedford Gardens, of getting close to Ruth, because she was afraid the woman might die?

"Well." Hannah led the way under the willow trees. "None of us know how much time we or anyone else has left. It's part of life, right? Reaching out. Making the best of things."

Charlotte agreed.

"I think you're the perfect person to help out at the nursing home right now." Hannah wiped her hand over her forehead as she spoke. "If you keep it to two hours a day, it should be manageable, right?"

"That's what I've been thinking too." She would be helping other people, and that would be good for the kids to see.

"Maybe the children could help you with some of the activities," Hannah said.

That was an idea; although, honestly, Charlotte couldn't imagine any of them wanting to help at Bedford Gardens, and forcing them certainly wasn't something she wanted to take on because requiring them to do their chores and keep up with their homework was already more than enough.

AFTER LUNCH CHARLOTTE HEADED into town, intending to stop by Mel's Place for a cup of coffee. Instead she drove through downtown and didn't stop until she had reached the nursing home parking lot. Maybe Oscar Smith was in Bedford today. She could tell him in person instead of over the phone. She stepped out of the bright sunshine into the dim lobby, which was surprisingly cool—and dark. Why weren't the lights on? Why were all the drapes closed? And why was music playing?

She squinted. The furniture was all pushed back, and several figures hobbled around in a circle.

"Charlotte!" It was Ruth's voice. Charlotte squinted more. Red's arms were around Ruth. Was she ill again?

"Did you come to join us?" Ruth asked, spinning around.

"What are you doing?" Charlotte asked.

"Waltzing." Ruth smiled. "What does it look like?" Ruth laughed as Red dipped her, and then said, after she righted herself, "It feels more like a dance hall if it's not so bright in here."

How could Ruth go from being rushed to the clinic one day to dancing the next? "Should you be dancing?" Charlotte asked.

"Of course. What's life without dancing?"

Charlotte smiled. "Is Mr. Smith here today?"

"He's in his office."

A minute later, Charlotte knocked on the director's door.

It seemed like an eternity until Oscar appeared. He dangled his reading glasses as he greeted her. "Come in, come in," he said. "Charlotte, right?"

She nodded.

"Please sit down."

There was a stack of files on his desk, and he sighed as he settled down into his chair. "Have you made a decision?"

"I'll do it," Charlotte said. "As long as it's just two hours a day and just until you can hire someone else."

Mr. Smith nodded. "You haven't met our receptionist, Diane. She's been on vacation, but she'll be back tomorrow. And Louise, the nurse, will be on duty when you're there, plus her staff." He stood. "I'm going to wait until Stephanie knows whether her husband got the job or not to post the position."

Charlotte realized she'd been smiling since she'd entered the room. Was she that nervous?

"I won't be around much this next week," Oscar said. "I have an inspection coming up at the Harding nursing home." He stood. Obviously it was time for her to go.

"I've left a stack of books and paperwork for you on the receptionist's table. Please give your forms to Diane tomorrow. She'll fax them to me in Harding."

Charlotte took a step toward the door. He wasn't giving her much of an orientation. "What if I have questions?"

"Ask Diane. Or call me if you need to." He shook her hand and thanked her and then ran his hand through his gray hair. "Oh, and make sure you take the safety test online tonight. You'll need that completed before you start work. Let's make your first day Monday, all right? I think we've had enough excitement around here for this week."

She nodded. "Back to the safety test. Can you tell me more about it?"

"It's all in the emergency protocol booklet."

"Oh." Charlotte said good-bye, slipped through the door, and headed back into the dim lobby. The dancing had stopped but the music continued.

There were several binders on the desk—*Patients' Rights, Nursing Home Laws and Regulations, Infectious Diseases,* and *First Aid*. She picked up the stack along with two folders that had her name written on yellow sticky notes on them. The label on one read EMERGENCY PROTOCOL and the other read COGNITIVE AND DEVELOPMENTAL THEORIES FOR SENIORS. At the bottom of the pile were several forms.

"It looks like you have quite a bit of homework for tonight, deary." Ruth stood beside her.

Charlotte nodded.

"Will we see you tomorrow, then?" Ruth asked.

Charlotte shook her head. "Not until Monday."

"That's our bowling day," Ruth said.

"Bowling?"

"On the Wii, of course." Ruth smiled. "You didn't think we'd tucked a bowling alley away in here, did you?"

Charlotte chuckled. To be honest it wouldn't have surprised her.

Chapter Seven

As Charlotte pulled into the driveway, Pete was on his way out. He slowed his pickup to a stop and rolled down his window. "I'm going to go help Dana in her classroom. She has some posters she wants hung on the ceiling."

Charlotte tried to imagine that and wondered if they would distract the students. She shook her head, trying to get rid of the image. Just thinking about it made her neck hurt. "Why don't you invite her to dinner? She probably hasn't had time to eat a decent meal all week."

Pete shifted into first. "I'll ask her. See you later."

Pete and Dana had been spending a lot of time together, but still it was unclear where they were headed. Pete didn't say much, even when Charlotte asked.

Sam's car was nowhere in sight as she pulled up to the house. Bob's pickup was parked by the shop though. Chances were that he was asleep in his chair. She climbed out of her car and grabbed the stack of binders and the folders. Fortunately her CPR and Red Cross first aid certificates were up to date. She kept those current year after year, in case Pete or Bob were injured on the job. It could make the difference between life and death on the farm until the paramedics arrived.

"I'm home," she called out, sliding the binders and folders onto the dining room table.

"I'm in here." Bob's voice came from the family room. "I made coffee," he said as she entered the room. His ruddy face, reddened by the summer sun, lit up, the wrinkles rising around his eyes and mouth. That was a real contribution for Bob. Funny, she didn't smell any coffee though. She headed into the kitchen. Sure enough, he'd forgotten to turn it on. She suppressed a giggle as she flipped the switch.

"It will be ready in a few minutes," she called out.

Ten minutes later, coffee in hand, they were chatting at the table when Christopher burst through the back door.

"We're home," he called out. His dimples flashed as he headed toward the fridge.

"Well," Bob said. "I think I'll go take another look at the carburetor on the combine." Charlotte knew that the hubbub of the afterschool rush got on Bob's nerves enough to send him out to his cave of retreat. "Feels like I've hardly seen you today, Char," he said, leaving his coffee mug on the table.

"Hi, Grandpa." Emily's voice was cheery as she came through the back door, followed by Sam. Bob grunted and kept going. "What's with Grandpa?" Emily asked.

"Nothing." Charlotte stood. "He just needs to get back to work."

Christopher bumped into Charlotte with the pitcher of milk.

"What do we have for a snack?" Sam asked.

Charlotte hadn't made cookies for a few days. "There are apples and plums," she said.

"Plums? We're supposed to eat those?" Christopher asked. "I thought they were just for Toby to play with." He poured a glass of milk and began rummaging through the pantry.

"Christopher, I plan to make jam with those plums."

"You do?"

"Of course," Charlotte said. "It's not right to waste them."

Christopher shook his head, obviously puzzled.

"What's for dinner?" Emily asked.

"I'm not sure," Charlotte said, peering into the refrigerator. And to think that she'd asked Pete to invite Dana out for dinner.

"Whose are these?" Sam asked, looking confused as he pointed at the stack of binders and the folders on the table.

"Mine. I need to do some studying and then take an online test."

"What for?" Sam started looking at the titles.

"For my temporary job."

Christopher spun around, spilling milk onto the floor. "You have a job?"

"A temporary one, at the nursing home."

"Whoa, Grandma." Sam sat down at the table.

"It's just two hours a day. And just until the director hires someone else to fill in until the activities director returns—or until someone else is hired to take her place."

Emily pulled out a chair and sat down too. "Eeew. That place is so depressing."

"It's not that bad," Charlotte said. "In fact, I'd like the

three of you to stop by sometime. I don't think the residents see many young people." She looked from Emily to Sam to Christopher—from one wrinkled, upturned nose to the next.

CHARLOTTE OPENED the oven door, turned the pork chops over, and then scooped some of the apple and sauerkraut mixture onto each one.

"Grandma, do you mind if Arielle comes out to dinner?" Sam held the phone against his chest. "Her dad's working late and her mom's in Harding."

Charlotte counted the pork chops. She had ten in the pan. "As long as you don't have seconds, we're fine."

"Thanks." Sam put the phone back to his ear and walked back into the family room.

"I need the computer," she called out after him. "And we'll eat in half an hour."

She gathered the binders and folders from the table. While Christopher did his homework, she'd reviewed the history of the company and the safety protocol. It turned out that Oscar Smith worked for a company that owned and operated nursing homes all through southern Nebraska and northern Kansas. It was the equivalent of the corporate farm. It seemed that locally run nursing homes were becoming a thing of the past.

The safety protocol was all common sense. Don't attempt to move a resident who has fallen. Call the staff nurse. Call 911. Don't assist the residents with their medications unless trained to do so. Check charts for food interactions before serving residents food. She wondered if anyone had done that with the food served at the tea yesterday. It hadn't even entered her head that one of the residents could have a medication reaction or a food allergy.

She sat down at the computer with the notebook and went online. She had to type in the Web-site address three times before she got it right. A password was listed in the notebook to log her in, and she felt nervous as she entered it. What if she failed the test? It took two tries with the password to get in and then she had to search the Web site for the safety test. She clicked on the personnel button and then searched that page. There it was in the lower left-hand corner. She clicked onto the safety-test button just as Pete came through the back door.

"How long until dinner?" he called out.

"Twenty minutes," Charlotte answered, standing.

"Hello, Charlotte." Dana stood beside Pete in the doorway to the family room. She wore slacks and comfy shoes, and her dark hair was twisted in a knot on top of her head.

"Oh, hello, Dana. I'm so happy you could make it." Charlotte glanced back at the computer, afraid the page would disappear. "I need to finish something up here, and then I'll be right with you."

"Come on," Pete said. "Let's go feed the horses."

"Would you ask Emily to set the table first?" Charlotte asked, settling back down in the computer chair.

Pete yelled up the stairs to Emily, and a minute later the back door slammed. Charlotte typed in her name and Bedford Gardens and then answered the first few questions with no problem. They were all from the reading.

"Grandma, I need the computer." Emily stood behind her.

"Set the table, please. If I'm done soon you can get on before we eat." Charlotte answered several more questions including one about evacuating residents to the parking lot in case of fire; she clicked on NEXT before she decided that she should have clicked ACROSS THE STREET instead. She intended to hit the back button to make the correction, but instead hit the CLOSE button.

Oh, dear.

She opened a new browser window and clicked back to the site, quickly moving through the buttons.

"The table's set. And dinner's ready," Emily said, stopping behind Charlotte.

"Just a minute." When Charlotte got to the test site again, it was obvious that her answers hadn't been saved. "Oh, good grief," she said.

"What's the matter, Grandma?" Emily asked.

"I accidentally lost the test. Now my answers are gone." Charlotte held her hands to her face. She didn't have time to start over now. Maybe she was too old for this job.

AFTER DINNER, Charlotte served chocolate ice cream on the porch to the kids and to Pete and Dana, and raspberry sorbet to Bob. The grown-ups sat on the porch chairs, and the children sat on the stairs, Sam and Arielle side by side, then Emily down a couple of steps, and Christopher at the bottom.

"Arielle," Emily said. "What did Mr. Santos say when you talked with him about college?"

Charlotte quickly glanced at Sam and noted the dirty look he shot Emily.

"So far I've decided to apply to Harding State, the University of Nebraska, and Midwest Lutheran," Arielle said.

"What do you plan to study?" Dana asked.

"Nursing." Arielle had seemed a little shy all evening and Charlotte wondered if it was because Dana was over or because she still felt bad about being in the house with Sam on Monday.

"That's a great profession," Dana said.

"Charlotte, didn't you want to be a nurse?" Bob asked.

She nodded. "Yes, I did." She was surprised that he remembered.

A minute later Arielle told Sam she should get going, that she had homework to finish up, but she would be back on Saturday morning to ride. She'd cleared it with her parents. Then Dana said she needed to go home too. After everyone said their thank-yous and good-byes, Charlotte scurried around, putting away the food and cleaning up the kitchen while Emily fed the chickens. Emily finished first and was on the computer by the time Charlotte headed into the family room.

"Honey, I need to finish that test."

"But you said I could get on after dinner." Emily turned toward her grandmother. On the screen was the homepage for the Parsons School of Design.

"Emily." Charlotte felt her impatience growing.

"Okay, okay. But don't hit the CLOSE button this time." Emily shut down her window and stood nearby.

"I need you to go tell Christopher it's time for his bath."

"I don't know where he is."

"Look outside." Charlotte logged back onto the Web site and clicked through the steps.

"Hey, Grandma, can I have a turn?" Sam asked. Was he back from taking Arielle home already?

Charlotte shook her head.

"I want to sign up for soccer in Harding."

"What do you want to do?" Bob stood in the doorway of the family room with the *Bedford Leader* in his hand.

"Soccer. In Harding."

"What have you found out about colleges?" Bob asked, settling down into his chair.

Sam crossed his arms. "That's all anyone talks about around here. Maybe I don't plan to go to college."

"Sam." Charlotte spun around in the chair.

"I don't get it," he said. "Neither of you went to college."

"Do you plan to farm?" Bob asked.

"Maybe." Sam ducked his head.

Charlotte bit her tongue. That was unlikely. If he wanted to farm he would be out working on the farm more. Besides, who knew what the future of the farm was and if it could support another person?

"Talk to me about trying out for that soccer team after you've done some research on colleges, son," Bob said.

"Then I need the computer. To look up colleges."

"I have to finish up this test first," Charlotte said. "And then Emily wants to look at colleges." Her words sounded a little ridiculous, given that Emily was three years away from graduating.

Sam rolled his eyes and plopped down on the couch,

and Charlotte turned back to the computer and the first question, which was different than the first time she took the test.

"Char."

She turned back toward Bob. He was standing in the middle of the room, the newspaper still in his hand, patting his pockets. "Have you seen my reading glasses?"

"No," she snapped, turning back to the computer. Did anyone care about what she needed to get done?

She couldn't even remember what she'd just read. She moved the cursor toward the BACK button and accidentally hit the CLOSE button again instead.

Chapter Eight

"Come on, Emily." Sam stood at the door of the chicken coop. "She'll be here in fifteen minutes." He'd woken up at six, nervous about the day because as he was headed to bed last night Emily had declared that she didn't plan to go riding with him and Arielle today after all. He'd pointed out that she was the one who had invited Ari to ride, but she just smirked and ducked into her bedroom.

What if he made a fool of himself? He felt like such a fraud riding horses.

Emily yawned and swung the egg pail gently back and forth. "You barely paid attention when I showed you how to saddle the horses the other night. And you said you didn't need me to show you how to ride—that you'd figure it out today."

"But why won't you come with us?" Sam wailed. He never imagined Emily not coming along.

"I'd just be a third wheel." She yawned again, a big fake one, and she failed to cover her mouth. "Besides, I was thinking about doing some research on colleges since

Grandma finally finished using the computer. Or maybe I'll go back to bed." She gave him one of her airhead looks and pushed against the gate.

He put his foot out.

Emily pushed back against the gate. "Samuel Slater, stop being such a jerk." A red hen squawked and flew up against the coop.

He crossed his arms. "Emily." Even Sam could hear the whine in his voice. "I can't remember how to put the saddle on the horse. Do you swing it over the right side or the left?" Now he was nearly screeching, but he didn't care. "And I don't think the horses like me." Not to mention he had no idea where to ride.

As Emily pushed harder against the gate, the hen squawked and fluttered her wings again. "I'm not even going to talk with you until you let me out of here." Emily pushed her weight against the gate as Sam removed his foot. She came crashing through, the chicken fluttering after her, both of them screaming. Emily tumbled to the ground, but the chicken flew up against Sam, its feathers beating his face. He batted at the hen and began jumping around in a circle.

"Close the gate!" Emily yelled, still clutching the pail of eggs, although three had rolled onto the ground, and one had broken.

He lunged against it just as a group of hens rushed the opening.

"Now help me," Emily said, leaving the pail, scrambling to her feet, and slipping on the broken egg as she took off across the driveway after the chicken. In just a few steps

Sam passed her and dove for the hen, wrapping his hands around her dusty middle and then sliding into the gravel.

"Don't kill her!" Emily hollered.

Sam rolled over onto his back, groaning as he lifted his elbow that was gouged by the gravel. A trickle of blood made its way down the back of his arm. The chicken struggled against him, trying to flap its wings and peck him in the chest at the same time. He groaned again. *Stupid chicken.*

"What's going on?" Grandma called out. Sam tilted his head to the side. A sideways Grandma stood by the back door, wiping her hands on her apron.

"Sam let one of the hens out." Emily glared at him as she picked up the pail and the two unbroken eggs from the ground.

As Sam clamped down on the chicken and rolled to his feet, he heard car tires rolling over the gravel. Sure enough, there was Arielle in her dad's pickup. Early. She rolled down the window. "Sam, you're bleeding." Her hair was braided, and she wore a cowboy hat. Her blue eyes shone with concern.

"It's nothing," he said, but he couldn't help but let out a groan at the timing of her arrival.

Emily waved at Arielle and Grandma started across the lawn. Arielle parked and Sam opened the gate to the coop and tossed the hen back in, and then Emily checked the gate after him to make sure it was latched.

"Thanks, Em," he muttered in a sarcastic tone.

She rolled her eyes at him.

Arielle hopped down from the pickup as Grandma

reached the driveway. "Are you going to go riding with us, Mrs. Stevenson?" Arielle asked.

Sam tried to brush the dirt off the back of his T-shirt. "Would you, Grandma?" *Please? Pretty please?* He hoped he didn't look too desperate, but he really needed someone to go with them. He was almost ready to ask Pete, even though he knew his uncle would say he had too much work to do.

"Emily, aren't you going?" Grandma shaded her eyes against the low sun.

Emily gave Sam another airhead look. "Oh, I wasn't so sure, but if you're going I'll go."

A DANGLING LIMB of a willow tree brushed against Sam as he tried to balance on Ben, but he kept sliding forward. Emily had made him cinch the saddle himself, but he wasn't sure if he had gotten it tight enough. He'd heard Pete tell stories of horses puffing up their bellies when they were saddled and then dumping their riders later when the saddles shifted, sometimes sliding all the way down. Sam jiggled the horn with his hands. It didn't feel that loose.

Emily rode ahead on Shania, the pure black mare and the liveliest of all the horses, leading the way down along the trail that led down to the creek. He turned his head. Grandma rode Tom, and beside her Arielle rode Britney. Sam wondered what they were talking about.

Grandma and Emily both said Britney was the gentlest of the horses. She was definitely the oldest. He turned forward again just as another willow limb brushed against him. He ducked for the next one.

The trail widened along the creek and Sam slowed, hoping Arielle would catch up with him and ride beside him, but she kept on riding beside Grandma. He could hear their conversation now.

"So why didn't you become a nurse?"

Sam had to concentrate to hear Grandma's answer. "I ended up getting married instead. Three years of nursing school—that's what it would have been back then—seemed like too long to wait."

"How come you couldn't have done both?"

Grandma paused. "Well, I never considered doing both, actually. There was so much to help with on the farm that I can't imagine I could have gone to school too. And then I got pregnant with Bill not too long after we got married."

Sam blushed and dug his heels into Ben. Boy, women sure talked a lot. In a couple of minutes he was even with Emily and in a moment of weakness decided to try to make peace with her.

"Thanks for coming along," he said.

"Actually, I was just teasing you earlier. I wouldn't have missed it for anything." She shot him a sarcastic smile from under the brim of the ratty old cowboy hat she had on.

He shook his head. "Stop messing with me."

"I like Arielle." Emily must have done something because Shania started trotting. "And you're pretty entertaining—especially when she's around. Why wouldn't I have come?"

Sam struggled to keep up. "Hey, could you wait for Grandma? So maybe I could ride with Ari?"

Emily looked over her shoulder. "They're way back there. How about if we stop at the meadow?" At that Shania began to trot.

"How do I make Ben go faster?" Sam called out as he dug his heels into the horse. Ben turned his head from side to side.

"Giddyap, Ben!" Emily called out and the horse took off, trotting along the creek, bouncing Sam up and down and back and forth in the saddle all at once.

Five minutes later they all stopped in the meadow and gathered around Emily.

"This is so much fun," Arielle said, taking off her hat and tucking a loose strand of hair behind her ear. She bent forward and rubbed Britney's neck.

Sam slid off Ben and then stumbled as he hit the ground.

"Sam, we're not stopping." Emily turned Shania toward him.

"I need to check my saddle." Sam leaned down and undid the girth. As he tried to cinch it again, Ben sidestepped. "Hey, boy." Sam pulled Ben's head back and patted the gelding's flank. "Take it easy." The horse snickered and Sam re-cinched the girth. He wasn't sure it was any tighter than before, but he didn't want to ask Emily to check it, not in front of Arielle.

Emily and Grandma started on ahead, and Arielle pulled up next to Sam. They rode quietly for a minute and then Ari started to tell Sam about what Grandma had said about the nursing home. He tried to look like he was interested. It had taken Grandma two days just to figure out how to do an online test so she could start working at the nursing home, and it wasn't like she was even working. Not really. It was only temporary.

"I'm thinking about volunteering there," Arielle said. "During seventh period, instead of doing study hall. It would look really good on my nursing school applications."

Sam leaned back in his saddle. If she volunteered at the nursing home seventh period, could he still give her rides to the pharmacy after school?

"What do you think?"

He smiled at her. "Sounds great."

"What about you? You could volunteer too." She held on to the reins with one hand. Already she was more comfortable than he was. "What do you think?" she asked.

Sam turned to look at her just as the trail turned and began to rise. He was really bummed that she wasn't going to be in study hall but not bummed enough to want to volunteer at the nursing home with her. Still, he started to say, "Yeah, that sounds—" But his saddle began to slip. "Like—" Ben jerked forward, stumbling against a rock. Sam leaned forward, grabbing at the horse's mane as the saddle began to slide. "Uh-oh—" Sam slipped to the side along with the saddle.

"Get your feet out of the stirrups!" Emily yelled from the top of the hill.

Somewhere, in the distance, Grandma shouted, "Sam!"

He was falling headfirst. But, obeying Emily for once in his life, he slipped his feet from the stirrups as Arielle jumped down from Britney.

He landed on his back on the trail with a thud, and then his head hit the ground. He couldn't breathe. He couldn't move. Ben walked away slowly, a few steps up the hill, the saddle hanging lopsided against his belly.

"Are you okay?" Arielle was down on the ground beside him.

"Yeah," he said, stretching out his legs.

He turned his head and saw Grandma's boots sliding down the hill.

"I think it just knocked the wind out of him," Arielle said, looking up at Grandma.

"Okay. Do you feel like you can sit up?" Grandma's hands were on his shoulders.

Sam nodded, took a deep breath, and sat up. A second later he stood.

At the top of the hill, Emily re-cinched Ben's saddle. "You had it two notches too loose," she called down as he shuffled up the hill, taking shallow breaths. Ben raised his head and let out a neigh. Sam scowled at the gelding. The horse raised his head up and down and then from one side to the other as if he were laughing.

A HALF HOUR LATER they stopped again, this time at an abandoned homestead. An old windmill spun in the breeze, and a loose piece of metal flapped against the weathered wood of the falling-down barn.

"I have lemonade and sugar cookies," Grandma said as she turned her attention to her saddlebag.

Sam slid off Ben. Lemonade and sugar cookies seemed like a really quirky snack, but he didn't care. He was happy Grandma had thought to bring some food along. Emily came around from the other side of the barn and dismounted, dropping Shania's reins. Sam did the same with Ben's, but wondered if it was wise.

"Don't we need to tie them up or something?" Arielle asked.

Emily shook her head. She looked like she was trying to keep from laughing. "They'll be fine."

The morning sun was beating down now, and they gathered in the shade of an old gnarly tree.

"So, Arielle," Emily started. "What are you going to do after you become a nurse?"

"Oh, I don't know." Arielle helped herself to another cookie and broke it in two. "I guess I'll work for a while, and I'd like to get married at some point along the way."

Grandma smiled.

Arielle glanced at her watch. "Uh-oh, it's already eleven."

Sam jumped to his feet, relieved that the conversation had ended. "We'd better go back. I need to head out to the airport this afternoon."

Sam climbed onto Ben. He hoped Arielle wouldn't want to go on any more rides in the future. One was definitely enough for him.

Chapter Nine

Charlotte pulled into her temporary parking space at the nursing home. It was one o'clock Monday. At one thirty the residents would begin bowling on the Wii. Charlotte had never played on a Wii personally, but Ruth had assured her it was very simple. Basically Charlotte only needed to be there to supervise and break up any arguments.

Arguments? Charlotte had felt a little alarmed. Ruth said that some of the residents took their bowling games very seriously but it had never come to blows. Charlotte grabbed the binders off the passenger seat, climbed out of the car, straightened her denim skirt, and headed into the nursing home.

A woman at the front desk frowned at her.

"You must be Diane," Charlotte said.

She nodded. "It's about time you got here," the young woman said. Her auburn hair was in a side ponytail, and she wore heavy eyeliner and a light blazer. She looked to be in her late twenties.

"Pardon?" Charlotte asked.

"We expected you hours ago." She drummed her long red fingernails on the counter.

"I only work two hours in the afternoon." Charlotte signed her name in the employee logbook and took a deep breath.

"Is that all you're going to work?"

Charlotte nodded.

"Most people work extra. Stephanie always did. Eight hours a day even though she was only paid for four."

Charlotte picked up her notebooks. "Well, I'm very part-time and very temporary—that's my agreement with Mr. Smith."

Diane stared at her but didn't say anything, and Charlotte walked toward Stephanie's office. She sat down at the desk, pulling up Stephanie's calendar on the computer, leery that she might accidentally erase something important. The woman was organized, that was for sure: Monday, August 27. Stephanie had planned to do the newsletter in the morning. *Newsletter?* Did Oscar Smith expect her to do a newsletter? She stood and walked back across the lobby.

"Diane, is Oscar in?"

"No."

"Will he be in today?"

Diane shrugged. "Call him and find out. His phone number is in your Rolodex." She turned back to her computer and without looking at Charlotte said, "And you can call me too, to ask me stuff like that. Or send me an e-mail. You don't have to walk all the way across the lobby."

Charlotte retreated back to her office. Why would she call or send an e-mail when she could ask in person? And if Diane expected e-mails from her, someone would have to show her how to use the e-mail program.

She looked up Oscar's number and dialed it. She immediately got his voice mail and left a message about the newsletter. Maybe she shouldn't have called so soon. Surely she'd have a couple more questions before the afternoon was over.

As she started up the stairs to the activity room, Diane called out, "Hey!" Charlotte stopped. "We have a volunteer coming in this afternoon. You'll need to orient her."

Charlotte took a step back down the stairs. "Orient her?"

"Yeah. That's part of Stephanie's job."

Charlotte started to protest but stopped herself, turning back toward the staircase. It was probably Arielle. That would be easier than working with someone she didn't know. And besides, if Arielle was at the nursing home when school ended she would be less likely to end up out at the farm with Sam before Charlotte had a chance to get home. Having Arielle volunteer at Bedford Gardens could have all sorts of benefits.

She would ask Ruth what volunteers usually did, but still she needed to talk to Oscar; he couldn't expect her to do in two hours a day what Stephanie did in eight.

Red stood at the top of the stairs. "We've been waiting for you," he said, leading the way to the activity room, shuffling along in his fleece-lined slippers, even on this hot August day. The light from the fluorescent bulbs overhead bounced off his shiny head.

The room was packed with residents, the TV was on, and the Wii symbol was in the middle of the screen.

"Good afternoon, Charlotte," Ruth said from the edge of the room. "Welcome to your new job."

"We're very grateful to you for filling in for Stephanie," Red added.

As the residents all settled onto the couch and the folding chairs, Charlotte asked Ruth how she was feeling.

"*Shh,*" Ruth said, smoothing out her skirt. "If there's one thing I insist on, it's people not asking me how I feel."

Charlotte felt her face flush. She hadn't meant to offend Ruth.

"Let the games begin," Red called out, the controller in his hand. With the push of a button, a bowling alley appeared on the screen. "Ladies first." Red passed the controller to Betty. "To our reigning champ." He gave her a little bow.

Charlotte knew from the notes she had read that Betty had early dementia, but the woman functioned quite well. Charlotte stepped back toward the corner and Ruth followed her. They sat down side by side on two folding chairs.

"I didn't mean to be brusque with you, deary, just a minute ago." Ruth placed her hand on Charlotte's arm. "You were the fifth person in two minutes to ask how I was feeling, that's all."

"Don't give it another thought," Charlotte said. The two watched Betty bowl her second ball and get a spare. Betty's Wii character had long black hair, but hers was completely gray, although still long. She was obviously an experienced bowler, taking a step forward and then tucking one foot behind the other as she swung her arm back and then forward, pushing the button that released the ball.

Red was next. Not surprisingly, his character had a head full of red hair and a red beard.

"Are you going to play?" Charlotte asked Ruth.

"Oh no," Ruth said. "I don't know that game at all. I have no idea how it works." She laughed. "Golf was what I played."

"There's golf on the Wii, right?" Charlotte was sure she'd heard that somewhere, maybe from Christopher.

"That's what Stephanie said. You know, it's her Wii. Anyway, we were going to do a little exploring into the golf game, go out for a round." Ruth smiled. "That was before the baby arrived."

"Maybe we can figure it out," Charlotte said, and then immediately regretted it. She could barely figure out how to take a test on the Internet, let alone a Wii game. She kept on talking. "We have a volunteer coming in today. What do they usually do around here?"

"We haven't had many, to be honest." She twisted her wedding ring. "I imagine a volunteer could read to Aggie or help Red with his puzzle."

"How about you?" Charlotte asked. "Could a volunteer help you with anything?"

"Me? Oh dear, no. I'm getting by just fine," Ruth said.

"Ruth, it's your turn," Red joked.

She waved him off with a laugh.

Charlotte sat up straight. Maybe Arielle knew how the Wii worked! That would be ideal.

"Stephanie was going to teach Red how to play baseball on the Wii too," Ruth said. "He used to be a semi-pro player."

"Really?" Charlotte had a hard time imagining that.

"He's shown me the photographs to prove it," Ruth said.

Charlotte smiled, wondering what Ruth's story was. When had she come from England? Had her husband been British too? When had he died? Was Red as crazy about her as it appeared?

"Do you have children?" Charlotte asked the older woman.

"No. I was never blessed that way."

"I'm sorry," Charlotte said, regretting that she had asked.

"Oh, don't be. The good Lord has blessed me in other ways."

Charlotte shifted in the hard chair, unsure if she should ask Ruth more questions.

But the older woman continued on without another prompt. "He's blessed me with other women's children, most recently Stephanie's little one." She paused for a moment and then added, "I began delivering babies during the war."

Charlotte guessed she meant World War II. "Well," she said, "that explains why you were so calm the other day."

Ruth nodded. "I lived in London and had just graduated from nursing school. We were short of doctors, of course. I seemed to have a knack for delivering babies, and soon the other nurses were calling me Baby Doc." Ruth smiled. "I was all of nineteen."

The first four bowlers finished their game and the next four took their positions.

"In April of 1947 I was moved out of that clinic, though, and into a hospital dedicated only to soldiers. That was where I met my Arnie."

"He was a soldier?"

"Yes," Ruth answered, "an American GI. He looked a little like Fred MacMurray."

An image of the father from *My Three Sons* flashed through Charlotte's mind.

"Just a regular American man. At the time I just thought his back was injured."

"So you were a war bride," Charlotte said.

Ruth smoothed out her skirt. "Yes. One of one hundred thousand from the United Kingdom." Her gaze fell toward the door. "Oh, my. That was so long ago." For a second she was silent, and then she said, "Well, look at this precious young thing."

Arielle stood in the doorway, squinting into the room. Her hair was pulled back in a tidy bun, and she wore a pink blouse and a pair of blue capris. "Hi, Mrs. Stevenson," she said.

After Charlotte introduced Arielle to Ruth, she took her to Aggie and suggested that she read to the woman. "I'd rather bowl," Aggie said in a clear voice.

The game was winding down with Betty as the winner, and the residents were beginning to leave the room.

"I can show you how to play," Arielle said, her voice filled with excitement. "No problem."

Aggie beamed and scooted her wheelchair forward to the middle of the room. Arielle started a tutorial for Aggie and placed the controller in her hand, wrapping her own around the woman's. "Okay, the trick is to line up your person and then pull back." Arielle guided Aggie's arm. "And then push this button as you swing your arm forward."

Aggie grinned from ear to ear as her virtual bowling ball lumbered down the middle of the virtual alley.

"Arielle," Charlotte said, "what do you know about Wii golf?"

"Well," she answered, turning toward Charlotte, "I've never done it, but I know I can figure it out."

A HALF HOUR LATER, Charlotte stopped at Red's puzzle table with Arielle right behind her.

Arielle shook Red's hand and then tilted her head to look at the puzzle. "It looks like Ireland," she said.

"Right you are," Red said, smiling down at the landscape photo of the village and river.

"Are you Irish?" Arielle asked.

"Right again. I grew up in Boston, but my grandparents lived in Ireland, in a village along the Shannon River, much like this photo." He sat back down in his chair. "I visited them a few times. Even went to London once." Red sighed. "I'd like to get to Florida to visit my son, but I don't travel much anymore." He held out his hands. "This arthritis almost crippled me a decade ago." He wiggled his crooked fingers. "It's also in my back and knees, but it's a little more under control now."

Arielle asked him what he took for his pain, and Red answered, "Too many pills. And you don't want to hear about the side effects." He chuckled. "Would you like to help me with my puzzle? I can find the pieces—I just can't always fit them into the right place."

"Mrs. Stevenson, is that all right?"

They were done with the tour, and Charlotte couldn't think of anything else for Arielle to do right now. They'd decided that Arielle would teach Ruth Wii golf in a day or two. "Sure," she said.

Arielle sat down next to Red just as Ruth approached the table. "I'm ditching you for a younger woman," Red said and then laughed.

"Good gracious," Ruth said. "It's about time."

Charlotte started to say her good-byes, but then Ruth pointed out the window. "Look," she said. "There's a young man in the parking lot with a soccer ball."

"It's probably my—" Charlotte and Arielle said in unison.

"Grandson," Charlotte said.

"Friend," Arielle said.

Ruth clapped her hands together. "Oh, good. I was hoping that one of you would know him."

Sam kicked the soccer ball across the pavement. Charlotte craned her neck. Christopher was with him and so was Emily.

"All three of my grandkids are out there," Charlotte said.

"Oh, do invite them in." Ruth started for the staircase.

Arielle stood. "Sam said he would give me a ride to work." She turned toward Red. "I'll be back tomorrow to help you with the puzzle."

A minute later, Charlotte, Arielle, and Ruth were all at the front door of the nursing home. The grandchildren came into the lobby, Sam holding the soccer ball, and Charlotte introduced them to Ruth. They said hello but looked uncomfortable.

"So you play soccer?" Ruth asked Sam.

"Yes, ma'am," he answered.

"Football is what we called it back home."

"Are you from England?" Sam asked.

"Yes. From London. Chelsea is my team—I went to my first match in 1936."

Sam had a look of disbelief on his face and Ruth chuckled.

"Dear boy," she said, "the club was founded in 1905. Still," she sighed, "I may be one of their oldest fans."

Sam said he was partial to Manchester United, and a look of mock horror crossed Ruth's face.

"Just kidding," Sam said. "But I do like Newcastle."

Christopher wandered toward the staircase. "What's up here?" he asked his grandmother.

"Residents' rooms." There were five assisted-living studio apartments, but only Ruth's and Red's were occupied. "And the activity center—where they play cards and the Wii."

"They have a Wii?"

Charlotte nodded.

"Wow." Christopher gazed up the stairs.

"It belongs to the activity director, the one who had the baby. But she's left it for the residents to play."

"May I play it?" Christopher turned back toward his grandmother.

Charlotte smiled and shook her head.

"We'd better get going," Arielle said. "Or I'll be late for work."

The children said good-bye to Ruth.

"I'll be home soon," Charlotte said from the doorway of Bedford Gardens. "Tell Grandpa. And Emily, please set the table." She blew the children kisses as they piled into Sam's 240-Z.

"Well, you have certainly been blessed," Ruth said, closing the door behind the children. "How many children and grandchildren do you have?"

"Five grandchildren and another on the way." Anna was due in December. "And three children," Charlotte said. It was hard to know how to answer that question anymore, but yes, she still had Denise, even though she was in heaven. "Two boys who are living, and a daughter—Sam's, Emily's, and Christopher's mother—who died almost a year and a half ago now."

"Oh, Charlotte," Ruth said. "I am so sorry."

"Thank you," Charlotte said. Tears sprang into her eyes. She felt the blessing of Denise though. It was far better to be grieving for the rest of her life than never to have had her daughter and now her grandchildren.

Chapter Ten

On Wednesday the heat from the asphalt parking lot burned through the thin soles of Emily's flats. She crossed her arms as she watched Sam tug on a wire under the hood of his car. "Is this going to take very long?" she asked.

Sam muttered something.

"Pardon?" she asked.

He muttered again.

"Samuel Slater, I can't understand a word you're saying." She leaned forward.

He pulled his head out from under the hood and yelled, "I don't know!"

Emily jumped backward. "No need to shout," she said.

"No need to nag," he countered.

"Maybe we should walk to the nursing home," Christopher said, appearing from the back of the car where he'd been sitting on the bumper. "Since the bus already left."

"Sounds like a good idea," Sam said, and then he stuck his head back under the hood.

He had no idea what he was doing. "Let's go," Emily said, pulling on Christopher's hand.

A few minutes later they turned onto Main Street.

"It's hot," Christopher said, swinging a stick back and forth as he shuffled along. His backpack was slung over one shoulder, hanging halfway down his back. Why hadn't she told him to leave it in Sam's car?

"Not any hotter than at the farm, and you play outside there for hours." Emily slowed down her pace. Lucky for Arielle it was her day off at the pharmacy and it didn't matter if she was stuck at the nursing home. Emily wrinkled her nose. She couldn't believe how depressing that place was. How did they all stand it? She was never going to get old.

Christopher dropped the stick and picked up a small branch that had fallen from one of the trees that lined Morley Park. Emily's book bag felt heavy, and she could feel sweat trickling down the back of her knee. The shade from the towering trees was hardly making a difference.

"Why don't you call Grandma and ask her to come get us?" Christopher dropped his backpack down on the grass.

"We're almost there," Emily said, and then, in an attempt to distract her little brother, asked him when he was going to meet with Rick Barnes to ask him about writing articles.

He shrugged. "Grandma is supposed to call him." He stood, grabbed his backpack, and started to walk, dragging the branch behind him.

"Oh." *Well, good luck with that,* Emily thought. Here it was Grandma's third official day of her new job, and she was already really distracted.

They reached the medical center and then jaywalked to

Bedford Gardens Convalescent Center, as the sign said. *Convalescent*. Was there a more depressing word in the entire English language?

That was what had been so nice about doing housework for Miss Middleton during the summer. The woman lived in her own house, not some depressing home. It wasn't old people that Emily had a hard time with, obviously; it was when they were forced to live in a tacky place like Bedford Gardens.

The landscaping around the building was a disgrace too; in fact it was practically nonexistent. Christopher started to run, jumping onto the sidewalk. Wasn't that just like him? Complain, complain, complain, and then take off like a chicken with its head cut off. She quickened her step, but she was so tired and sweaty that she didn't think she could run if she wanted to.

She pushed through the front door and stopped abruptly. The lobby was full of tables with little old ladies and men sitting around them, and Arielle and Grandma were both serving tea. Christopher settled into a chair next to Ruth, the woman they had met on Monday.

"Emily," Ruth called out. "Here's a chair for you too." She pointed across her table to an empty seat. Emily concentrated on not wrinkling her nose. She had thought Grandma would be ready to go home. She made her way to Ruth's table and sat down as Christopher filled his plate. A woman sat in a wheelchair on the other side of Ruth. She looked pretty feeble and just had a bowl of pudding in front of her, but the other people seemed in pretty good shape.

Emily looked around the lobby. The carpet was worn

and the eggshell walls needed to be repainted. Too bad *Extreme Makeover Home Edition* wasn't in the habit of tackling places like this.

A stocky woman with a stethoscope around her neck walked up to the table and started talking with the old woman in the wheelchair.

"That's our head nurse, Louise," Ruth explained.

"But she's not dressed like a nurse," Christopher said. The woman had on a pair of polyester pants and a flowery blouse.

"You're right," Ruth said. "She doesn't need to for what she does. She oversees our medications, tracks our blood pressure, listens to our lungs, all of that. If there's a problem, then we're transferred to the acute-care section of the nursing home or to the clinic."

"Oh," Christopher said.

Grandma approached and asked if Ruth wanted more tea.

"Oh, please," she said. "If you would be such a dear."

Emily grimaced a little as Grandma poured the tea. So, basically, it seemed like Grandma was working as a babysitter, or maybe a waitress. The nurse knelt down as she talked with the woman in the wheelchair, and Emily couldn't tell what she was saying, but she knew it was important. Why hadn't Grandma gone on to college? She would have made a really good nurse.

There was a commotion toward the back of the lobby and Arielle squealed, "Mrs. Stevenson!"

"Excuse me," Grandma said, all calm and collected.

Emily strained her neck to see what was happening.

Arielle stood next to a woman with a walker who had just wandered into the lobby.

"Am I supposed to clean it up?" Arielle was asking.

The nurse stood, held up a walkie-talkie that hung around her neck on a string, and spoke quietly into it.

Grandma was whispering to Arielle, and Emily couldn't hear her answer, but then someone showed up and helped the woman with the walker down the hall toward the other wing.

"She has Alzheimer's pretty bad, poor thing," Ruth said. "Connie will take care of her."

Emily took a sip of her tea as Christopher shoved cookie number three into his mouth.

EMILY RETREATED to the corner of the lobby with her history book after the tea was over, but in no time Grandma had found her. "I really need your help," she said. "The tea got started almost an hour late, and I need to make sure everything is cleaned up before I can go home."

"I thought there was a tea last week." Emily closed her book with a thud.

"There was."

"Then why another one this week?" she asked.

"Because the women enjoyed the one last week so much." Grandma sounded annoyed. "This was a scaled-down version, just store-bought cookies and tea. It gives them a chance to dress up and visit."

Emily rolled her eyes. Like they needed a tea to do that. They could dress up and visit all day long if they wanted to.

Christopher was already scurrying around, collecting

teacups. Emily reluctantly joined him. She shuffled into the kitchen with a stack of plates in her hand. Ruth was at the sink, rinsing dishes. "Many hands make light work," she said and then added, "Thank you, Emily. You are a dear."

Emily straightened her back and smiled.

"And there's that older brother of yours." Ruth nodded toward the doorway.

Emily turned. Sam, looking all sweaty, walked into the kitchen carrying a stack of plastic water glasses. He must have ended up walking too.

"Did you get your car started?" Emily asked.

"Nah. I'm going to see if Pete will come in with me after dinner." Sam put the glasses on the counter. "Hello, Miss Ruth," he said. "How are you today?"

"Fine, but I was wondering, dear, could you help rinse these dishes? I'd best sit down for a few minutes."

When Emily came into the kitchen with another stack of plates, Sam and Ruth were talking about English soccer. "So Chelsea is your team?" Sam asked.

"For over eighty years." She sighed. "I went to that first match with my father. Then I hauled my American husband to one before we left England. He'd played a little soccer in the army, but had never seen it played like that. And it seems like they just keep getting better."

"That Frank Lampard is really something," Sam said.

Ruth's eyes twinkled. "Isn't he? Did you see the goal he had against Man U?"

"I read about it online. We don't have cable." Sam added more dish detergent to the water, and the suds began to grow.

Emily shook her head as she returned to the lobby for

another load of dishes. She wasn't used to hearing Sam have a conversation with someone, not like that, and especially not with an old person. Grandma was arranging the vases of flowers on the receptionist's desk, but the woman sitting there didn't seem very happy about it. When Grandma first told them about her job it had seemed like she was going to be in charge, but it didn't appear that way at all now.

The third time Emily entered the kitchen, Ruth was asking Sam where he planned to go to college.

"I haven't gotten that far yet," he said. "But I'm thinking about playing club soccer in Harding this fall."

"Not unless you get serious about looking at colleges," Emily said.

"Oh?" Ruth turned her petite little body on the stool.

"Grandma and Grandpa both told him that planning for college is a priority over trying out for a soccer team." Emily placed the dishes on the counter. "But he hasn't done a thing."

"I will," Sam said.

"Of course you will," Ruth said. "College is your future. One must always be planning ahead and taking the initiative."

Emily hurried back out to the lobby and began collecting the tablecloths. She hoped they were almost done. Arielle headed toward the kitchen with two teapots.

"Ask Sam to come fold the tables," Grandma said to Emily.

"He's washing dishes." Emily took off for the kitchen, right behind Arielle.

"Here's your friend," Ruth said to Sam. Sam turned and

blushed. Ruth stood. "I'm fine now. Let me finish up the dishes."

Emily stopped for a moment. "You know, this china is really beautiful. It's the nicest thing they have at this place."

"Why thank you, dear." Ruth carefully stacked the plates in the rack. "It's mine. I brought it from England all those years ago."

Emily picked up a clean cup from the dish rack. It had a simple pale pink pattern of roses around it. And the china felt nearly as thin as paper. Why would Ruth let her china become part of Bedford Gardens?

EMILY, CHRISTOPHER, and Arielle were all crammed in the back seat of Grandma's Ford Focus for the ride to Arielle's house. Emily sat in the middle as still as she could. She was too hot to touch anyone else.

"That was fun," Arielle said.

"Except for when that poor woman needed her diaper changed," Emily said, wrinkling her nose. "I know one thing for sure—I'm not cut out to be a nurse."

"Honestly," Arielle said, "I don't know if I am either. I want to help people, but—"

"Well, don't make a decision based on that," Grandma said, pulling the car out onto Main Street. "There are lots of different kinds of nursing."

"Well, let me tell you," Christopher said. "The school nurse has to deal with that sort of thing all the time. Did I tell—"

"Christopher," Grandma interrupted.

He wiggled around. "Okay, okay. Hey, I had a lot of fun today at the nursing home," he said, now shifting in his seat and bumping Emily. She cringed. "Can I help out again, Grandma?" he asked.

"I think so," she answered. "Wednesdays are the day I need the most help."

"Speaking of help," Arielle said. "Red was telling me he's having problems with his insurance. They don't want to pay for the pain medication he needs."

"Did he talk to the social worker?" Charlotte asked.

"Who?" Arielle leaned forward.

"The social worker. Her office is on the acute-care side. That's what she does—makes sure the residents get the services they need."

"Oh." Arielle sat back against the seat. "That sounds like a fun job."

Emily wanted to laugh. How could Arielle think any job at the nursing home sounded like fun?

Grandma stopped in front of Arielle's ranch-style house on the edge of town. Her mom's station wagon was parked in the driveway, but her dad's pickup wasn't around. From what Arielle said, his job as a deputy meant a lot of late hours.

Sam hopped out, walked Arielle to her door, and waited for her to go inside. Then he turned and jogged quickly back to the car.

Emily yawned. She was ready to be home. "Grandma, did you start dinner before you left?"

"I'm trying a new recipe in the Crock-Pot, bean enchiladas."

Emily smiled, wondering what Grandpa and Pete would have to say about that.

She wondered what they were having at the nursing home for dinner. What did vegetarians in nursing homes get to eat? Probably lots of pudding. The place was dismal. Emily tilted her head. Except for Ruth. There was something special about her. She reminded Emily a little of Miss Middleton. But how did Ruth stay so positive living in a place like that?

Chapter Eleven

Charlotte put the last of the lunch dishes into the dishwasher and then glanced at the clock as she washed her hands: *12:40*. She needed to get going. It was Friday, her last day of work for the week. She'd intended to get another load of laundry done so she didn't have as much to do over the weekend. "Bob," she called out, drying her hands, "could you hang up the clothes that are in the dryer?"

"Bob." She stopped in the doorway to the family room. He sat in his chair, his reading glasses on his chest and his eyes closed. "Bob?" Was he faking it? He let out a snore.

She hurried into the laundry room and took the clothes out of the dryer, spreading them on top, one on top of another, hoping she could hang them up, unwrinkled, when she got home.

TWENTY MINUTES LATER she sat in Stephanie's office at the nursing home, staring at the blinking light on the phone. Surely it meant she had a message. But how did she listen to her messages?

She headed out to the lobby and asked Diane.

"You punch in your password." Diane drummed her fingernails on her desk as she spoke.

"I don't know the password."

"But you've been working here for—how long?"

"This is my fifth day."

Diane shook her head and began leafing through a notebook.

"This is my first message." Oscar still hadn't called her back about her newsletter question. Maybe it was from him.

"Here it is. Stephanie's password is seven-eight-nine-four."

"Thank you."

Charlotte headed back to her office and picked up the phone, punched in the number, and listened to the message. It was Oscar. "You can do the newsletter," he said. "Or Diane. It doesn't matter to me."

Well, that wasn't very helpful. Charlotte stood. Diane would have to do it. There was no way she had the time. She headed back across the lobby.

"You know you can e-mail me, right? Or call?" Diane said, squinting at Charlotte.

Charlotte nodded. Arielle had helped her figure out the e-mail system. "But I need to talk with you. Oscar left a message saying that either of us could do the newsletter, but I don't have—"

"What makes you think I do?"

"You work full-time."

"So?"

"Diane, you're going to have to do the newsletter. Talk to Oscar if you have any questions." Charlotte turned and headed for the stairs before Diane could respond, pleased that she'd said what she needed to say. She walked quickly into the activity room. Red and Ruth were playing rummy with another couple, and four other residents were playing cribbage.

"How is everyone?" she asked.

All eight of the residents looked up and smiled, but then refocused on their games. Aggie and Betty sat in the corner with Connie, who was reading to them from a book of poetry.

Charlotte stepped back, not wanting to disturb them, and went back to her office to read more of the manuals. Maybe she shouldn't have passed the newsletter on to Diane, but this was the first day she'd had any extra time.

When Arielle arrived, Charlotte suggested she go upstairs and see if Ruth wanted to learn to play Wii golf—she hadn't felt up to it earlier in the week—or if Connie wanted her to take a turn reading to Aggie and Betty.

At two thirty, Charlotte checked on everyone again. Red, Ruth, and the other residents were still playing cards, and Arielle was reading to Aggie while Betty dozed in her chair.

Charlotte told everyone good-bye. Her plan was to catch Christopher before he took the bus home. She'd finally remembered to call Rick Barnes this morning, and he had agreed to talk with Christopher before he needed to leave for Richfield for the football game.

Charlotte retrieved her purse from her office and hurried by the receptionist desk, waving at Diane.

"See you Monday," the young woman called out.

"Monday?" Monday was Labor Day and her elder son Bill and his family were coming over, just like they did every year.

"For our annual barbecue." Diane sounded impatient. "It's on the calendar."

Charlotte hugged her purse close. "Oscar didn't say anything about it."

Diane ignored her. "The activity director organizes the barbecue." Now Diane sounded exasperated.

"I can help," Arielle said, coming down the stairs.

"Do you need Stephanie's phone number?" Diane was already writing on a notepad. "Call her. She had everything all planned out. You'll just need to oversee it."

Charlotte took the piece of paper and said thank you. Arielle gave her a sympathetic look and then said, "Sam will be here pretty soon. He's going to give me a ride home since I don't work this afternoon. And Emily is riding along."

Charlotte nodded, appreciative of how well Arielle communicated. Charlotte wanted to ask her if Sam had talked with Mr. Santos, the school counselor, about college but knew better than to pull Arielle into the middle of things. Sure, she might encourage Sam to get moving, but it wasn't her responsibility.

RICK BARNES LOOKED UP from his computer and over his reading glasses as Charlotte and Christopher walked through the front door of the *Bedford Leader* office.

"Good afternoon," he said, standing and shaking Charlotte's hand and then Christopher's. "I was just working on the layout for next week's paper."

"You do the layouts too?" Christopher asked.

Rick chuckled. "I do a little bit of everything."

The office was on the first floor of an old brick building with high ceilings. A framed copy of the first *Bedford Leader* hung high on the wall. Charlotte stepped closer to read the date. *1880.* A collection of historic photos circled the open room. A Model T on Main Street. A horse-drawn thresher and raggedy-looking crew in a wheat field. A group of ladies in long, white dresses holding parasols posing in front of the library. And there was her father's theater, circa 1950. Charlotte smiled. Rick Barnes was continuing a fine tradition.

She turned back toward Rick and Christopher. "Here," Rick said. "I just started using InDesign to do the layouts. I e-mail the docs to my printer in Harding, and he ships the newspapers back here. The turnaround time is less than twelve hours."

"Wow," Christopher said. "It takes us a whole month to get our paper out, and there are ten of us."

"What do you do?" Rick asked. "Layouts? Writing?"

"I'm supposed to be working on an article, but I'm having a hard time coming up with an idea." Christopher shifted from one foot to the other. "Grandma said I need to come up with a subject that has to do with the school or Bedford or something."

"That's good advice," Rick said. "You always have to keep your audience in mind. For example, I would never write a feature story about someone who lived in Lincoln, unless that person had a strong connection to Bedford. Everything I write about has to do with Bedford."

"Oh," Christopher said, shooting a look at Charlotte. She tried not to smile.

"What's going on at your school right now?"

"A lot of sweating, mostly."

Rick laughed. "Over the course work?"

"No, over the heat," Christopher answered.

Rick smiled and then asked, "Does the school have air conditioning?"

"No."

"You could write about that," Rick said. He reached for a yellow legal pad on top of his oak desk. "I should keep this list on my computer, but I do it the old-fashioned way. I keep a running list of story ideas. If someone tells me about a new person in town, I write that down. Or maybe I read an article in another paper or online, and I get an idea about something that is going on in Bedford that I can write about. Or maybe I'm doing some research about something I'm interested in and I come up with an article from that." Rick dropped the pad onto his desk. "What interests you, Christopher?"

"Well..." He shot another look at Charlotte. "Besides the usual stuff, I'm interested in our dog Toby and tornados and the weather." He scratched his head. "Stuff like that."

"Well, there could be an article idea somewhere in there," Rick said as he patted Christopher on the shoulder.

CHARLOTTE WAITED UNTIL BOB had fallen asleep in his chair after dinner to call Stephanie. She took the cordless phone out into the backyard and dialed the number written on the piece of paper. Christopher walked along the corral fence, Toby at his side.

The phone rang and rang, and Charlotte was just about ready to hang up when Stephanie finally answered. Charlotte apologized for disturbing her and asked about the Labor Day barbecue.

"Oh, that," Stephanie said. "I'm sorry, I forgot to tell you." She explained that the nursing home had been having the barbecue for years, according to the woman who'd had the job before her. The cook hauled in a gas grill and barbecued hamburgers and hot dogs. They had a few activities.

"Games?" Charlotte asked.

"Yeah." There was a long pause. "It seems like someone mentioned a watermelon-seed-spitting contest."

"Really?" Charlotte wanted to laugh.

"That's what I was told." Stephanie sounded really tired. Perhaps she'd been napping.

"Would it be okay if my family came with me?" Charlotte asked. Maybe Bob and everyone would be willing, this one time. "We usually have a Labor Day barbecue at Heather Creek Farm."

"That's a good idea, actually. Just tell the chef how many extra people to expect."

Charlotte thanked Stephanie and said good-bye. She wanted to ask what Stephanie's long-term plans were but figured she would have said if she knew.

Charlotte ended the call and then stood there, still holding the phone in her hand. What would make a barbecue at Bedford Gardens fun for the kids? Charlotte swatted at a mosquito as Emily, wearing cowboy boots with her shorts, came out of the barn. It was a look that would appear ridiculous on most people but looked stylish on Emily. Her raggedy cowboy hat, the one that had been Pete's, was tilted to the side with her blonde braids trailing behind.

Charlotte smiled. Square dancing would make it fun for everyone. The younger people could dance and the residents could watch.

"Who were you talking to?" Emily asked as she approached the lawn.

"Stephanie."

"The woman who had the baby?"

Charlotte nodded.

"What about?" Emily asked.

"The Labor Day barbecue at the nursing home." Charlotte opened the back door.

"I thought Uncle Bill and his family were coming here." Emily followed Charlotte into the house.

"They are." She needed to think through the square dancing idea before she said anything.

"So, you're not going to be here, or what?" Emily took her hat from her head, hung it on a peg on the back porch, and planted her hands on her hips as she sashayed into the kitchen.

"I thought we could all go to the nursing home." Charlotte placed the phone in its cradle. "It would be good for all of us—and the residents."

"Grandma!" Emily wailed in the same tone Denise had used all those years ago. "You're kidding." She said it like a statement, not a question. Clearly she thought it was bad idea. "What are we going to eat, pudding?"

Charlotte wanted to say that at least that would be

vegetarian, but she stopped herself. She'd better call the cook in the morning to see what was on the menu. If vegetarian burgers weren't included then she'd need to take one for Emily.

"Grandma!"

Charlotte turned toward her granddaughter. "Emily, I still need to talk to Grandpa and Bill, but I think that's what we'll do."

Emily wrinkled her nose and spun around, her hands still on her hips, and flounced into the family room.

Charlotte smiled as she followed her granddaughter. She might as well reveal the best part of the plan. "And I thought we'd have square dancing."

"Square dancing?" Now Emily was wailing.

"What's with you?" Sam's voice was loud, too loud, as he twirled around in the computer chair.

"Ask Grandma." A moment later, as Charlotte settled into her chair in the family room, she heard Emily's boots on the staircase.

"What's up?" Sam asked.

"Let me talk to Grandpa," Charlotte said, picking up the notebook next to her chair.

Bob let out a snore.

"Later," Charlotte said, picking up a pen. "Then I'll fill you in." First she wrote down "seed-spitting contest" and then "four watermelons." That should be enough. They could have the contest out on the patio. Next she wrote down "square dancing" and then "where?" She tapped the pen against her cheek. The outdoor patio would be the best place for the dancing too; it could be a sort of *Dancing with the Stars* at Bedford Gardens.

Chapter Twelve

"That's the dumbest idea I've ever heard of," Emily said as she rode with Grandma into Bedford on Saturday afternoon. "Dancing at the nursing home? Some of them can barely walk."

"Emily."

"It's true. Do you think they'd really enjoy a dancing contest? There's no way any of them can still dance." Emily turned up the air conditioning. Grandma was out of her mind.

"As a matter of fact, some of them do still dance. But for this event the residents would watch. The rest of us would dance."

Where did Grandma come up with these ideas?

"Who knows how to square dance anymore anyway?"

"They used to teach square dancing in school." Grandma pulled into Herko's Grocery. "Don't they still?"

"No." Emily couldn't imagine having to learn how to square dance. She wasn't exactly sure what it was, but she thought the women wore those hokey skirts that poofed out all funny.

Grandma pulled into a parking space. "I just need to figure out the music for the square dancing."

"What about the food?"

"The nursing home ordered it. Stephanie had requested it before Lillian was born. I'm just picking up the watermelons."

Emily led the way into Herko's. Grandma acted as if her temporary job were some big deal, but it wasn't like she was doing any more than she did at home. She was taking care of other people, doing chores, and planning dinners. That was all.

The big box of melons took up half the produce section. "We need four of these," Grandma said as she began thumping them.

"What for?"

"The seed-spitting contest."

"The what?" Emily stepped back. What was Grandma talking about?

"Just what I said." Grandma lifted a melon into the cart.

Boy, things were getting weird. Emily halfheartedly thumped a watermelon.

"There will be forty of us altogether," Grandma said.

"But how many of them can eat watermelon?" Emily thumped the biggest melon in the box, even though she probably wouldn't be able to lift the thing.

Grandma thumped a smaller watermelon. "I think anyone who can still eat can eat watermelon." She picked one up.

Emily lifted another one—not the big one, but still it nearly toppled out of her hands. She held on tightly and rolled it into the cart with a clang.

"Careful," Grandma said, gently placing another one in the cart.

As Grandma stood in line at the checkout, Emily thumbed through a new copy of *Elle* magazine. She stopped at a sweater dress with a huge cowl neck. Who would ever wear something like that?

"Emily," Grandma said, "I'm almost done." Then she handed her card to Sally Meyers, the nosy checker with the big hair and the rhinestones stuck in her fake nails. They looked like she did them herself from the kits they sold in the beauty section of the store.

"Wow," Sally said, pushing her feathered hair away from her face. "Four watermelons. You must be planning quite an event."

Grandma only nodded. She moved to the end of the conveyor belt and began putting the watermelons back into the cart.

"I hope they're good watermelons," Sally said as Emily tried to slip through the line to the other side of Grandma. "You never buy that many."

Grandma swung the cart around. "They're for the nursing home barbecue on Monday."

"Really?" Sally leaned on the conveyor belt. "My great-aunt Aggie lives there."

"Oh," Grandma said. Clearly she hadn't known Aggie was related to Sally.

"They're so good to her there. She's really happy. And you know, that makes me happy." Sally stood up straight and started picking at the nail on her left index finger. "She wasn't happy living on her own, that's for sure. Bedford Gardens has made all the difference."

Emily turned toward Sally. Was she serious?

"I just love my aunt Aggie. I just saw her yesterday. Did

you know she used to be a chemist?" Sally shook her head as she smiled. "Obviously the smarts in the family skipped me."

Emily took the cart handle and began pushing it toward the door as Grandma said good-bye to Sally. Aggie didn't do much but sit in her chair, although Grandma did say she played the Wii the other day. Emily couldn't imagine it though.

The doors slid open and Emily pushed the cart through. What if Grandma ended up like Aggie someday? Or worse, like the woman with the walker whose body still worked, kind of, but whose mind was long gone. Emily shivered, even though the heat of the day was nearly suffocating. She didn't want to think about her grandparents getting old like that.

Grandma clicked the button on her key remote, which made the trunk door magically rise. "Well, isn't that something that Sally and Aggie are related?" Grandma lowered a watermelon into the trunk. "I must have known that but forgotten it."

Emily let out a groan. Miss Middleton, even though she was like ninety or something, never forgot things.

"What's wrong?" Grandma said, slamming the trunk closed.

"You're forgetting things. You act like you're getting old." Emily opened her door, and in a second both she and Grandma were fastening their seat belts.

"Emily, I *am* getting old." Grandma started the car.

Emily groaned again. "Please don't say that."

ON SUNDAY EVENING before youth group started, Ashley asked Emily what she was doing for Labor Day.

Emily slumped down into the overstuffed couch in the fellowship hall. "A barbecue at Bedford Gardens. Grandma's making me."

Ashley sat down beside her, her auburn curls bouncing with the motion. "Oh. I was hoping you could come over to our place. Dad's going to grill."

"What time?" Emily asked.

"Four."

Emily threw up her hands. "That's the exact same time as the nursing home barbecue. Grandma says the residents have to eat early so the heavy food will digest by bedtime."

"Well, it sounds like fun. And like a really good service-oriented type of thing."

Emily frowned. Ashley could sound so grown-up at times. "Hey." Emily sat up straight. "Do you want to come help with it? We're going to do square dancing—or try to anyway." If Ashley thought it was such a good idea, how could she pass up the opportunity for her own community service?

"Could Mom and Dad and Brett come?"

"Sure," Emily said, hoping that would be okay. "But you might need to bring some of your food, to make sure there's enough."

"I'll ask Mom," Ashley said as Jason Vink, the youth pastor, started to strum his guitar. "She loves to square dance. She'd think it was a hoot."

Emily smiled. Having Ashley at Bedford Gardens would definitely make tomorrow a better day.

Jason kept strumming. "You know God has a plan for each of our lives. He tells us that in Jeremiah 29:11: '"For I know the plans I have for you," declares the Lord. "Plans to prosper you and not to harm you, plans to give you hope and a future."'"

Emily sat up straight. *Hope and a future.* Every once in a while, stuff from the Bible sounded so poetic, so beautiful, so promising. Did God really have a plan for her? Sure, she could see Him planning for her to go to Haiti to feed hungry kids or to become something she loathed, like a nurse or something. But could He actually have plans for her to do something she wanted to do? Like go to New York to study fashion design?

Jason continued talking. "He calls all of us to different things. God made us to enjoy beauty and to create. Remember that as you pursue your dreams. He wants us to serve others, but that can happen in all sorts of ways." He started to play the first few chords of a song on his guitar.

Ashley joined in as the group began singing. Emily exhaled slowly. Three years. Maybe in three years she would be in New York, enrolled in school, living out her dream.

"EMILY, YOU DID WHAT?" Grandma asked, standing in the middle of the barn, the milk pail in her hand.

"I invited Ashley and her family to the barbecue." Emily held two of the calico cats in her arms. "I forgot to tell you last night."

"Why did you invite them?"

"She asked me to her house. And her mom likes to square dance." Although that wasn't why she had invited the Givenses, but it could come in handy. What was with Grandma? Usually she was thrilled when Emily invited Ashley anywhere.

"Melody likes to square dance? Really?" Grandma paused for a moment. "Then I'll give her a call. Maybe she can help me."

Emily led the way out into the barnyard and veered to the left toward the corral to feed the horses while Grandma walked toward the house. Maybe she should have told Grandma the reason she asked Ashley was that she was stressed about helping with the barbecue, and having Ashley there, in all of her calm glory, would make it easier for Emily.

She had really come to appreciate Miss Middleton during the summer, so why did she hate the nursing home so much? No, the bigger question was, why did Grandma like it so much? And Christopher? That was what really puzzled her.

She grabbed the pitchfork and began tossing hay into the feed trough. Britney and Stormy headed toward her, walking slowly, switching their tails at the flies. She definitely wasn't a take-care-of-people kind of person. Sure, doing housework for someone was fine, but feeding them or bathing them or something like that . . . that was too weird.

Animals were one thing. People were another. Art and animals. Those were the things that made her happy. One of the hardest things about going to New York in a few years would be leaving the horses. How had her mom stood it all those years ago when she took off for San Diego? At least Emily knew what it was like to live in a city. Sure, New York was more crowded than San Diego, but it wouldn't be a total shock to her.

"Hey!" Christopher walked toward her, a yellow legal pad in his hands. "I'm looking for a story."

Emily leaned against the pitchfork. "A story?"

"Yeah. What were you thinking about?"

"New York."

"Oh." He stopped beside her. "Mr. Barnes said I needed to write about something that has to do with Bedford."

"Well..." Emily forked another load of hay into the trough, dumping strands on Stormy's face. "New York has nothing to do with Bedford."

"What do you think I should write about?"

Emily shrugged. "I don't know. You could write about the horses."

He wrinkled his nose until it practically matched his white T-shirt. "That's as bad as those stupid kitten articles. In fact, I think Natalie is writing an article about her neighbor's horse."

Emily stabbed the pitchfork into the bale of hay. "You know, I actually have no idea what you should write about." The last thing she needed to worry about was Christopher's article.

A half hour later she was sitting at the dining room table with a glass of ice water when the phone rang. "I'll get it," she yelled as she leaped from her chair.

It was Uncle Bill. "Oh, hi," she said. "I'll get Grandma." It had been a few weeks since they'd seen Bill, Anna, Madison, and Jennifer. She wondered how big Anna was with her pregnancy.

"Grandma!" Emily called out. It would be fun to have a baby in the family. She hoped it was another girl. "Grandma!" she yelled again.

"Down here." A second later the basement door opened, and Grandma held out her hand for the phone.

Emily sat back down at the table, not wanting to miss Grandma's side of the conversation. "Yes, that's right. I said that in my message."

There was a long pause.

"I know it's disappointing. But I have this job—although it's temporary—and I didn't find out until Friday that the barbecue is my responsibility."

Emily took a sip of her water, and Grandma headed toward the laundry room. Emily stepped toward the sink and refilled her glass. She could barely hear Grandma.

"But Bill, we would still really like to see you."

Then there was another long pause.

"Okay. Talk to Anna and let me know."

Emily scooted back to the table just as Pete came crashing through the back door. "Sam said we're not having our barbecue."

"That's right—I told you on Friday."

"Mom." Pete swooped his hat off his head. "You didn't. And I already asked Dana to join us."

Emily stood. No one wanted to go to the stupid barbecue except Grandma. She put her glass in the sink and headed down the hall as Pete pleaded with Grandma.

"There's nothing I can do," Grandma practically yelled as Emily began running up the stairs.

Chapter Thirteen

Charlotte pushed open the door to Bedford Gardens with her hip and staggered through, carrying a big cardboard box with two of the watermelons in it.

"So," Diane called out from the receptionist's desk, "did you figure everything out for today?"

Charlotte nodded. It was her fourth trip from her car to the nursing home, lugging in supplies. Diane hadn't offered to help with a thing.

A minute later, Charlotte surveyed the back courtyard area of the nursing home. It was perfect with its large concrete slab and the shade trees towering over the area. As she spread a red plastic tablecloth over the food table, she heard a sweet voice behind her.

"Charlotte, dear."

She turned. There was Ruth, coming through the patio doors, wearing a blue linen skirt, a white blouse, and a red-checked scarf around her neck. "How can I help you?"

Charlotte coached herself not to ask Ruth how she was feeling. "Your outfit is splendid," Charlotte said, suddenly aware that she was using one of Ruth's own words.

"Thank you, dear. What can I do to help?"

Charlotte nodded toward the stack of paper plates and napkins. "You could arrange those."

As Charlotte began spreading tablecloths on the round tables the staff had carted out to the patio, she asked Ruth if it was too hot for the residents.

"Oh, heavens no." She fanned out the napkins. "Some good old-fashioned warm air will do all of us good."

"Where did you have the barbecue last year?"

"Out here, I'm sure. But I was laid up then, from my broken hip, and wasn't able to participate."

"How long have you been here?" Charlotte asked.

Ruth cocked her head. "Just over a year." She laughed. "And I never intended to stay, mind you."

"Really?"

"Oh, no." Ruth sat down on one of the folding chairs. "I was visiting a friend here in Bedford, a woman I used to know in Montana, when I fell and broke my hip." She shook her head. "It was such an old lady thing to do, and until that time I was in total denial that I was old, traveling the country by myself, planning on finally going back to England. And then, while my hip was doing a fine job mending, I was diagnosed with congestive heart failure and stayed on in the nursing home. I really am better now, believe it or not, and I was so relieved when they opened the assisted-living studios a few months ago. It's been a godsend."

Charlotte had a million questions. "Who were you visiting?" Perhaps Charlotte knew the friend.

"Pearl Johnson—but she's since moved to Minneapolis to live with her youngest daughter, who happens to be a doctor." Ruth smiled with pride. "Pearl was a single mom with four boys and three girls in Butte, Montana, when my husband and I moved there. By the time we moved away, her children called me their second mom."

"Did you live in Butte before you moved here?"

"Oh, heavens no. I have a condo in downtown Seattle."

Charlotte stumbled against a chair as she spread the last tablecloth. "Seattle? What were you doing there?" She could not, for the life of her, imagine Ruth living in downtown Seattle, especially not in a condo.

"Well, that's where my dear Arnie died. We found a doctor for him there." She gazed past Charlotte, past the bank of azaleas and into the cement retaining wall that separated the Bedford Gardens property from the homes behind it. "He suffered greatly. Of course, we didn't know what from for years, not until post-traumatic stress disorder began to be discussed long after the Vietnam War. When the World War II soldiers came home, they were heroes. They went to college, had careers. No one guessed that the war hadn't ended on the inside for so many of them. Including my Arnie." She sighed and stood. "What else may I help you with?"

Charlotte pointed to the box of paper plates and cups. Ruth asked about Sam, and Charlotte began telling her about everyone who was coming to the barbecue, much to Ruth's delight.

She wished it were as delightful as it actually sounded. Bill and Anna had agreed, reluctantly, after a flurry of phone calls, but Pete refused to come. He was more than miffed that Charlotte had changed the family's plans.

Ruth turned away from the table. "I'm feeling a little spent," she said. "I'm going to go rest until the party begins."

BOB AND CHRISTOPHER were the first of the family to show up. Emily had decided to ride with Sam and Arielle, to Charlotte's disappointment. She had anticipated Emily helping her set up. Bob sat down in the lobby and began chatting with Red while Charlotte hustled Christopher into the kitchen to count plates and cutlery.

As Charlotte hurried out the kitchen door, Christopher, who was obviously fishing for a story, asked the cook what she liked the most about working at Bedford Gardens. "The pay," she hissed, pushing her hair back from her sweaty face.

Charlotte was tempted to duck back through the door to see if Christopher had a follow-up question, but she didn't have time for that. She hurried into Stephanie's office and pulled the square dancing CD from her purse, the CD she had borrowed from Melody. She picked up the CD player from the corner behind the door. She'd listened to the tape earlier in the afternoon and tried to recruit Emily to practice the moves so she could demonstrate, but Emily had flatly refused. Thankfully Melody and Russ were coming—they could model do-si-do and sashaying and bowing to your corner.

Charlotte's granddaughters Madison and Jennifer would probably enjoy the dancing, but she wasn't as sure about their parents. Charlotte found an outside outlet and plugged in the CD player.

"Mrs. Stevenson, what can I do to help?" Ashley slid the glass door closed behind her. The girl's hair was pulled into a ponytail and she wore blue capris and a white scoop-necked T-shirt.

Charlotte stood, straightening out her skirt. "Are your parents here?"

Ashley nodded.

"Oh good," Charlotte said. "Could you sweep off the patio?" Charlotte pointed to the area behind the tables where the dancing would take place. "The staff was supposed to do it but they've been shorthanded."

At least that's what it seemed like. Sometimes it seemed as if the staff moved in slow motion. That was probably better than if they were uptight and go-go-go; that would only make the residents nervous, but still, their slower pace was hard for Charlotte.

Ashley wrapped her hands around the push broom that was leaning against the outside wall of the building. "Where's Emily?"

"She's coming with Sam and Arielle."

"Oh," Ashley said and walked toward the far corner of the patio.

Charlotte felt a tinge of disappointment that Emily didn't seem as eager to be as helpful as Ashley was. In fact, Emily seemed determined to avoid the nursing home. If it weren't for Emily's fondness for Miss Middleton, Charlotte would be really worried. At least she knew Emily could be caring and compassionate toward an older person.

Twenty minutes later, when Sam, Arielle, and Emily arrived, Connie was shuttling the immobile residents out onto the patio. "Sorry we're late." Arielle approached Charlotte first. "Emily forgot her sweater, so we had to go back out to the farm."

Charlotte raised her eyes at her granddaughter.

Emily shrugged. "It might get chilly this evening. And besides, the sweater makes my outfit." The coral sweater was draped over her shoulders, the sleeves looped in front. Just looking at it made Charlotte feel the heat that much more.

Arielle began chatting with Red about his insurance claim. Ashley carried a huge bowl of potato salad through the door and placed it in the trough of ice that Christopher had filled, under the cook's direction, and then turned and smiled at Emily and said hello. Emily waved and backed up against the building.

In the rush of the final preparations, Bill, Anna, Madison, and Jennifer arrived. Anna, six months along, wore a floral maternity dress, and her pregnancy was starting to be more noticeable. The girls both had their hair in pigtails and wore matching sundresses. Bill crossed his arms and stood along the wall a few feet away from Emily. The girls ran up to Charlotte and gave her big hugs, almost knocking her off balance.

"Do you like our dresses?" Jennifer asked, twirling around.

"They're beautiful," Charlotte said, stepping back. She needed to check with the cook to see how long until dinner would be served.

"And our hair?" Madison asked, lifting up the red ribbon.

"Gorgeous!" Charlotte took another step away. "Did you see Emily over there? Next to your dad? Go show her your new outfits."

The girls hugged Charlotte again and skipped away. Charlotte gave Anna a quick hug and said, "I need to go check on things in the kitchen." As she hurried away, she was sure she detected a frown on Anna's face. Charlotte looked over her shoulder. Anna was marching across the patio toward Bill.

As she passed through the lobby, Charlotte saw Dana come through the front door of Bedford Gardens with Pete in tow. What were they doing here? Dana held up her hand in a wave.

Charlotte walked toward them. "Hi."

"We decided to join you," Dana said. She wore her hair in braids. "Pete said there was going to be square dancing. It all sounds like so much fun."

"Oh," Charlotte said. She hadn't included Pete and Dana in the number of extras she'd given the cook. She forced herself to smile. "I'm so glad you could come. Everyone is out on the patio." She pointed through the sliding door across the lobby. "We'll eat in a few minutes."

"Charlotte." It was Diane's voice. She stood behind the reception desk, her arms crossed. "How much family do you have?"

Charlotte shrugged and hurried toward the kitchen.

Ten minutes later, the meal was ready to be served, and Charlotte stood behind the table, greeting people and helping Connie oversee the residents, pleased with how well things were going. A breeze blew through the patio. It wasn't exactly cool, but it was refreshing.

"Come sit down, Charlotte," Bob said as he followed Red through the line.

"In a minute," she answered.

"How many burgers can I have?" Pete asked, ready to spear a second.

"Start with one, please," Charlotte said, giving him a smile.

Bill was right behind his younger brother. "Just one? They're a little puny, don't you think?"

Charlotte kept smiling, aware that her face was growing tired.

Bill put a burger on Madison's plate and then one on Jennifer's. The younger girl turned behind her to say something to her mother and as she did her plate tilted.

"Jennifer!" Charlotte called out, but it was too late. The burger tumbled to the ground.

"That's okay," Anna said. "Just get another one."

"AREN'T YOU GOING TO EAT?" Bob asked.

"Later," Charlotte mouthed. By the time Pete and Bill had seconds there weren't any hamburgers left. She intended to have some potato salad, but by the time she had finished making sure all the residents had their plates full, the kitchen staff was already clearing away the food.

Now Connie was administering the dinnertime medications as the servers finished clearing the tables.

Charlotte approached Melody. "Thank you so much for doing the square dancing," she said.

Melody turned toward her. "Should we get started?"

"In a few minutes."

"Oh, good," Melody said. "Ashley is going to help demonstrate the calls."

Charlotte felt the pang of disappointment again. Why was Ashley so eager to help and not Emily? How had Melody raised such a sweet daughter? The two girls sat beside each other at the table with Ruth, Red, Arielle, and Sam. Ashley was talking with Ruth, but Emily sat with her arms folded, the sleeves of her sweater still dangling over her shoulders.

Melody clapped her hands and the residents and guests directed their attention toward her. "Time for the dancing," she called out. "Ashley and Brett are going to demonstrate the calls." Melody looked around the group quickly. "Hey, Pete and Dana, why don't you help too?"

Pete was still eating his burger, since he'd taken seconds, and he spoke with his mouth full. "What is this? PE class, like, twenty years ago?"

Melody laughed. "You betcha, although much better than that."

Dana, with a smile on her face, nudged Pete. He shoved the rest of his burger into his mouth and shook his head. She nudged him again, this time harder. He wiped his hands on his jeans and shrugged. Dana stood and took his hand, pulling him to his feet. They walked to the front, followed by Ashley and a very reluctant-looking Brett. Melody explained do-si-do, and Pete and Dana faced each other and then walked around the other, passing right and then left shoulders, back to their starting positions. Pete was grinning, despite himself. Ashley and Brett copied Dana and Pete. Brett looked miserable, but Ashley smiled, her auburn curls bouncing on her shoulders.

Charlotte sat down next to Aggie.

"Don't they teach square dancing in school anymore?" the old woman whispered.

"I don't think so," Charlotte answered. If they did, Sam and Emily never complained about it the way Pete and Denise had. Charlotte glanced at Bill. He was smiling. Come to think of it, he'd liked square dancing.

Melody explained allemande right and left and then decided she needed two more couples to demonstrate it. Before she could ask for volunteers, Bill grabbed Anna's hand and started toward the front. Red glanced back at Ruth, but she shook her head. Charlotte was relieved. Ruth's health was the last thing she needed to worry about today. Red leaned over the table behind his and whispered something to Arielle. She nodded, and they headed toward the front too. Charlotte stood to get a better look. Melody had the four couples in a square and was directing the men to take their partner's left hand and do a walkthrough.

Ruth began clapping, and the other guests and residents joined in. Sam crossed his arms as he watched Arielle, and Emily yawned.

"Do you like to dance?" Ruth asked Emily.

"Not—" Emily paused. "—this kind of dancing."

"It's not my favorite either," Ruth said quietly. "But still, it's enjoyable. If I wasn't feeling under the weather, I wouldn't miss the chance to experience it."

Emily didn't respond.

"I like your outfit," Ruth said, obviously trying again.

"Thank you." Emily smiled.

"How is your design class going?"

"Good." Emily began talking softly about her fashion

project, and Ruth listened intently as the four couples kept demonstrating square dancing moves under Melody's direction. Finally they were ready to perform to the music.

"Promenade your partner," the caller on the CD sang out, and the dancers began skipping around the square.

Sam still had his arms crossed, watching Arielle and Red lead in a California twirl.

"Sam," Ruth said, "Chelsea has a game next Saturday. Would you like to come watch it with me?"

Sam shrugged.

"They play Man U. It should be quite a game."

"Man U is brutal," Sam said.

"Yes, they can be," Ruth replied. "But I think Chelsea is up to the task."

"Really?" As Sam leaned on the table, Red and Arielle approached.

"What do you say, Sam?" Ruth asked.

"To what?" Arielle put her hand on Sam's shoulder.

"To watching the Chelsea–Man U game next Saturday morning. You would be welcome too," Ruth added and then smiled at Arielle.

"Sounds like fun."

Sam's head bounced a little, like he'd said something, but Charlotte couldn't tell what.

Red sat down. "Your turn," he said to Sam. "My knee is acting up." As Sam took Arielle's hand and headed toward the dancers, Red sat down beside Ruth and patted her hand.

Melody called for a second square of dancers, and Charlotte hurried over to Bob and whispered in his ear, suggesting he ask Emily to dance. He smiled and leaned over to his granddaughter. She frowned but said yes. Jennifer and Madison joined in the fun, and Connie pulled in one of the kitchen staff members to dance with her while Melody and Russ finished out the square.

Charlotte stood against the building by the patio door and watched Emily smile as her grandfather spun her around. And then Sam and Arielle promenaded around their square, laughing as they passed Dana and Pete. Charlotte headed toward the kitchen to thank the cook. The barbecue had been a splendid success. They would have another half hour or so of dancing and then the watermelon-seed-spitting contest, but as she headed through the lobby, she heard a commotion on the patio.

Diane must have heard it too because she rushed out the sliding door. By the time Charlotte reached the patio, Diane was directing the residents and guests away as she kneeled down beside Red, who was sprawled out on the concrete.

"Call 911!" Diane shouted at Connie.

"No." Red struggled to sit up, but Diane pushed him back down. "It's just my knee. I stood and it buckled. That's all."

As Charlotte bent down beside the man, Diane said, "I have this under control. He needs to be checked out by a doctor."

"But he said it's just his knee," Charlotte answered.

Diane shook her head. "I think you've already done enough, Charlotte, encouraging a resident to dance on a hot night like this. We don't know it's his knee. It could be heatstroke or a heart attack or anything."

Charlotte shook her head.

"You've already been negligent enough," Diane said.

Connie stepped forward. "The ambulance is on its way," she said. Then she knelt down beside Charlotte. "When a resident falls, we have to transport them to the clinic."

"Oh." Charlotte didn't remember that from the manuals. She stood.

Red groaned. "Oh, for the life of me," he muttered. "Don't I have any say around here?"

Diane stood too. "I'll call Mr. Smith and let him know what's going on." She looked straight at Charlotte.

It wasn't like she'd made Red dance. Should she have discouraged him from it? Had she used poor judgment in having square dancing at all?

Ruth put her arm around Charlotte. "He's fine. You'll see. This will all blow over by morning."

Chapter Fourteen

Arielle approached Sam in the hallway before first period the next morning.

"How's Red?" she asked.

"Fine. Grandma stayed with him at the clinic until the doctor checked him out. His knee flared up from the dancing—that was all. Just like he said."

"Oh, good." Arielle smiled her to-die-for smile, and then laughed. "Do-si-do," she said, her arms crossed. Sam crossed his arms too and circled around her. It took him a minute to register Jake's laughter. A second later his friend purposefully plowed into Sam, knocking him against the lockers.

"Hey," Sam said, landing on his feet.

"Hey, yourself." Jake pushed up the sleeves of his army jacket, which looked way too hot to be wearing. It was going to be another scorcher. "What are you guys doing? Some new dance?"

Arielle put out her hand to Sam and pulled him to the middle of the hallway. He hoped he didn't look like he wanted to allemande or anything. He was never going to hear the end of it from Jake if she kept this up.

"We learned how to square dance," Arielle said, twirling under Sam's arm.

Jake groaned. "That sounds like torture."

"Oh no," Arielle said, dropping Sam's hand. "It's a lot of fun. We danced last night at the nursing home."

Jake leaned against his locker. "Nursing home? Are you kidding? Sounds like you had a memorable weekend."

"Yeah, well," Sam said, "I've had better." He pulled away from Arielle as he opened his locker. His face grew warmer and warmer as he dug out his notebook. He hoped Jake wouldn't say anything to Paul. He slammed his locker and looked up and down the hallway for Arielle, but she was nowhere in sight. Sam realized he'd forgotten his literature book and turned back to his locker to dig some more.

By the time he entered his senior English class, the first bell was ringing. Arielle sat in the middle of the room, not at the front where she usually sat beside him. Sam turned around, but he couldn't catch her eye. Jake came in just as the second bell rang and slumped beside him. "Care if I join you?" he asked.

Sam scowled.

An hour later Sam hurried to physics class, determined to get there before Arielle. He did, and by the time she arrived there weren't any other seats in the class. She sat next to him, and Sam smiled to himself. They were studying photons, and she had obviously done the reading because when the teacher said that photons act as both waves and particles and then asked for someone to give an example of a particle and a wave, Arielle raised her hand.

"Well," she said, "a ball is an example of a particle.

Like a pool ball or a soccer ball. And waves are pretty self-explanatory—like the waves in the Great Lakes."

Or the Pacific Ocean, Sam thought. He still didn't get photons. How could something with no mass affect everything from sunlight to telephones? He imagined an ocean wave of weightless soccer balls and then shook his head.

"Sam?" the teacher asked. "Do you have something to share?"

"No." Sam sat up straight. "I was just marveling at the wonder of all this."

He could hear Jake in the back of the room guffaw and then say, "That's our Einstein." Sam had never felt like such a dork.

After class he said he'd see Arielle at lunch, but she shrugged and said she was going to stop by Mr. Santos's office to pick up information on a college in Tennessee.

"Tennessee?" Sam said out loud, but she was through the door before he finished the word.

At lunch he sat by Jake; Emily stopped by the table, her yogurt in her hand. "I heard you and Arielle had a fight," she said.

"What are you talking about?"

"Ashley said she heard you're in the doghouse." Emily held her spoon in midair and gave him that ditzy look of hers.

"I didn't do anything."

Jake threw back his head and laughed.

Sam scowled. "What are you laughing about?"

"You dissed her in the hall this morning. Don't you remember?"

"What?" Sam tried to remember what happened in the hall besides his feeling humiliated.

"You said you didn't have fun dancing with her."

Sam stood, his tray in his hands. "I didn't say that."

Jake stood too. "You might as well have."

Sam brushed by Emily. What should he do now?

Arielle wasn't in yearbook class. He sat down at the same table as her friend Sarah, but Sarah wouldn't look at him. In a few minutes Halley sat down and asked where Arielle was. Sarah nodded toward Sam.

"Oh," Halley mouthed.

"She went to her internship early today," Sarah finally said. "She really likes volunteering at the nursing home." She said this loudly, but then the two girls just sat at the end of the table and whispered, so Sam went over to one of the three computers in the room and started loading the new software. That was the only reason he was taking the class—the teacher said he could be the technical-support person. Arielle had talked him into taking the class for that very reason.

What if she never spoke to him again?

AFTER HIS SEVENTH-PERIOD STUDY HALL, Sam found Emily in the hall and told her she and Christopher needed to take the bus home.

She rolled her eyes at him in that ultra-annoying way of hers. "Good luck," she said. "I heard she's really mad."

"Em," Sam said, "please." His heart sunk. He hadn't meant to insult Ari, and, honestly, the barbecue had been a lot of fun, especially the square dancing after Red had finally given Sam a turn.

He pushed through the front door of the high school into the sweltering afternoon heat. He squinted as he rushed down the cement stairs.

"Hey!" Jake called from atop his skateboard at the edge of the parking lot. "Got your board?"

"Nope," Sam yelled back, lying. He veered toward his 240-Z and called out over his shoulder, "Besides, I gotta go."

"Go where?" Jake rolled toward Sam.

Sam pretended he didn't hear his friend. Jake knew where he was going. And besides, he didn't want him to look in the back of his car and see his board.

"Sam!" It was Christopher, coming across the lawn from the elementary school. "Wait!"

"You're riding the bus with Emily."

Christopher's face fell. Sam hated how his little brother did that so easily. He looked as if he'd just been abandoned, like he'd been told he was going to be dropped off at the boys and girls home or something. He didn't have time for Christopher's insecurities, not now.

Sam opened the driver's door and climbed in, turning on the ignition as he grabbed his seat belt with his left hand. He rolled down the window and backed out of the parking space.

"Good luck," Jake yelled and then began rolling, gaining momentum, as he neared the sidewalk. "Don't say something stupid." He crashed into the curb and went flying forward, across the cement and into the lawn. Sam waved as he went by and then glanced into his rearview mirror. Christopher was walking dejectedly toward the bus as Emily hurried to catch up with him.

Sam turned onto Main Street. Why did girls have to be so sensitive? Arielle hadn't acted this way before. Why now? The humidity was high, and he could feel beads of sweat form at his hairline. He was nervous enough as it was without having sweat pour out of every pore of his body. He swiped his arm across his forehead. He hoped he smelled okay.

He tried to think about something. *Soccer*. Two more weeks until the tryouts. But that made him nervous too. He had meant to set up an appointment with Mr. Santos today, but he'd forgotten. The stuff with Arielle had been too distracting. He turned slowly at the medical center and then pulled into the parking lot of the nursing home. Had Arielle walked over after fifth period? Or did she get a ride? Maybe her dad swung by and got her. He did that sometimes. Would she have told him about what Sam had said that morning?

Sam turned off the ignition, but he didn't open the door. What should he say? What if she wouldn't listen to him?

Why should she listen to him? He grasped the steering wheel tightly. Everything had been going so well. He could be such a jerk.

He bit his upper lip. Bedford would be worse than unbearable if Arielle wouldn't talk to him. It would be worse than it had ever been before. School. The farm. Not even soccer had any appeal without Arielle. He grasped the steering wheel tightly, as if he were holding on for dear life, and stared at the middle of the vinyl-covered wheel.

What if talking with her just made it worse? Maybe he should just pretend like nothing happened, just go to the farm and call her this evening about their physics assignment. It was about Einstein's photoelectric effect. Or just ignore her for a few days. She'd come back to him, apologizing for overreacting, right? Isn't that the way it was supposed to work?

He sighed. No. He might as well go in since he was here.

He slowly got out of the car, firmly slammed the door, and headed into the nursing home, adjusting his eyes to the dim lobby.

That woman, Diane, who always looked a little angry, was hunkered down in front of her computer screen. She didn't seem to notice him. *Invisible.* That was how he was feeling today.

"Sam." A voice came from the middle of the staircase.

Was it Arielle? he wondered as he looked up with a smile. No. It was Ruth, and she was coming toward him, just like a geriatric Energizer Bunny.

"There you are," she said, as if she were expecting him.

"We're having sundaes today. The cook forgot that Stephanie had ordered ice cream for the barbecue yesterday. Would you please come join us? Out on the patio?"

"Sure," he said again.

She linked her arm through his. What was with this woman? She talked funny and she acted funny too. As they walked through the lobby, Ruth said, "We're all a little tired from the party yesterday, I'm afraid, so we're only doing the sundaes as an activity today. But tomorrow we'll have our tea, which seems to have become a regular activity around here now. The men, though, are going to play baseball on the Wii tomorrow. Arielle showed Red how to do it this afternoon. Now baseball, that's an American game. Of course we have cricket in England, and I've never entirely understood baseball, but I enjoy watching it. Especially the Seattle Mariners. They were my home team."

Sam nodded. He was listening, kind of.

"Of course it pales compared to soccer. Don't you think?"

Sam nodded again as he opened the patio door. Ruth let go of his arm and slipped on through.

"That's why I'm really hoping you can come Saturday morning. You and Arielle—"

Sam looked up. There was Arielle at the first table.

"Isn't that right, Arielle?" Ruth said, sitting down beside her and motioning to the chair next to Arielle. "Don't you plan to come on Saturday morning?"

"I guess so," she said, glancing at Sam.

If she was coming, he was coming. He nodded his head, careful not to look too eager though. "Sure," he said. "I'd enjoy seeing a Premier League match."

"Well, good," Ruth said just as Grandma approached the table.

"Sam. What are you doing here? Arielle said her dad was giving her a ride home today."

Sam blushed. "I just thought I'd stop by." He wanted to say he'd had so much fun yesterday he couldn't stay away, but he couldn't get the words out. What was he supposed to say? That he wanted to see how mad Arielle was at him?

"Yeah," Arielle said. "My dad is coming back to get me. And right now I need to help Red fill out his insurance paperwork." She stood. "Guess I'll see you around—and on Saturday morning."

"I can pick you up," Sam said.

"The match starts at seven AM," Ruth interjected.

"I could come by at six forty-five." Sam stood too.

"Okay." Arielle slid open the door and turned her head toward him, just slightly. "See you then."

Chapter Fifteen

Emily watched Arielle sitting with her friends in the cafeteria the next day at school. Arielle was as friendly as ever to Emily, stopping to chat in the hall and smiling at her in the lunch line, but she was giving Sam the cold shoulder. Funny thing was that he didn't seem to get it. On the way to school this morning he said everything was cool, that he and Arielle were going to Ruth's on Saturday morning to watch a soccer match, that Arielle wanted to go, and he was going to pick her up. He told Emily she was imagining things.

"Go figure," she'd said to Sam. He was so obtuse.

Arielle threw her head back, laughing at something her friend Halley said. Emily searched the room for Sam. He sat all hunched over next to Jake and Paul. He looked like he was ready to slide under the table.

"Earth to Emily," Ashley said, standing with her tray. "Are you done?"

Emily nodded, folded her napkin, and placed it in her paper bag. She followed Ashley and tossed her yogurt cup into the recycling bucket. "Let's go see if we can hang out in the art room before class starts," she said to Ashley. "Maybe Ms. Carey left it unlocked."

"Do you think that's okay?" Ashley said.

Emily shrugged. "Let's just see." Ms. Carey seemed like she wouldn't mind. It was too hot to go outside. The old brick school stayed fairly cool, much better than the 150-degree steps or parking lot. They ambled down the hall, stopping by their lockers for their art supplies, and then arrived at the art room. Emily turned the doorknob. It was unlocked. She looked at Ashley and shrugged.

"You'd better knock," Ashley said.

Emily did and immediately a voice called out, "Come on in." Emily pushed open the door and both girls entered.

Ms. Carey sat at the back of the room, a yogurt container, a muffin, and a coffee cup on the desktop. "Oh, hi, girls."

Ashley nudged Emily.

Emily cleared her throat, suddenly nervous. "We were wondering if we could hang out in here—'cuz, you know, it's so hot outside."

"That's a great idea," Ms. Carey said. "Make yourselves at home. Go ahead and get started on today's lesson—it's on the board."

Emily turned toward the front. "Art service project" was written across the top of the white board in Ms. Carey's bold script. "Design a project to benefit a local nonprofit or service organization (think: church, park, Boy Scouts, Girl Scouts, food bank, nursing home)."

Emily stopped reading. Nursing home? Had Ms. Carey been talking to Grandma? Was there some sort of conspiracy going on?

"Due: two weeks from today." Well, that ruled out getting *Extreme Makeover* to come in for a complete do-over at Bedford Gardens.

"Cool," Ashley said. "This is a great assignment."

Emily winced. Sometimes Ashley could seem like the biggest goody-goody. Emily frowned. She'd thought they were going to be able to choose their own assignments. She'd wanted to design a line of winter clothes.

The girls sat down at their table and Ashley read the assignment again. "What do you think, Emily?" She took out her sketchbook and flipped it open. "What are you going to do?"

"Well, I know what I'm not doing. The nursing home."

"Seriously? I thought that would be a natural for you."

Emily grimaced. "How about you?"

"Well, I was noticing that the Sunday school classroom signs at church are kind of shabby. Maybe I could make new signs."

"That's a great idea." Ms. Carey was standing beside them. "That's exactly what I had in mind. I want you to experience how your art can change the world."

Emily groaned.

"Emily?" Ms. Carey walked in front of their table. "Do you have some insights about the assignment that you would like to share?"

Emily slouched. "How can a new sign change the world?"

"Oh, well, I didn't mean it literally. But art—beauty—does change the world in both little and big ways. We all need to do our part." Ms. Carey smiled. Her lip color was a perfect plum, and her eye shadow made her brown eyes shine.

Emily returned the woman's smile and sat up straighter. "Sure," she said, hoping she sounded convincing. What could she do? She didn't know any Girl Scouts in Bedford. Too bad Christopher wasn't in Boy Scouts. Maybe she could do something for the park. Like a sculpture or something.

Ashley had drawn the letters spelling NURSERY in her book in big, bold letters.

Emily pulled out her sketchbook and began designing a winter coat.

AFTER SCHOOL, Emily sat at the dining room table and sketched a pair of boots with four-inch heels. Why hadn't she thought of Ashley's idea? It was so simple and straightforward. And Grandma would have been really pleased that she'd chosen to do something that had to do with the church.

Everyone in the class except Emily had seemed to be able to come up with an idea. She was supposed to have it sketched out to show Ms. Carey by tomorrow. Maybe Ms. Carey wasn't as good a teacher as she pretended to be. Sure, Emily could see a service project like this at the end of the school year but not the beginning. And the idea that their simple little attempts could change the world? Who was Ms. Carey kidding?

Christopher slammed through the back door. "Whatcha up to?" he asked.

"Homework." Emily shaded the right boot.

"It doesn't look like homework." He tilted his head.

"Well, what do you know?" Emily regretted being so mean as soon as she saw his pathetic little face. Why did he take everything so seriously? "How about a cookie and a glass of milk?" she asked, trying to appease him and make herself feel better all at the same time.

He averted his eyes and then opened the refrigerator. A minute later he was sitting next to her, his elbow nearly touching her sketchbook. "Hey," she said. "Make sure you don't spill any of that. Or fling any crumbs my way."

He inched away from her. Why was Sam hiding in his room, moping, instead of playing with their little brother?

"What's for dinner?" Christopher asked.

Emily pointed to the Crock-Pot. "Go take a look." She'd been afraid to. Everything out of that pot tasted the same and hardly any of it was vegetarian. She'd eaten a grilled cheese sandwich every day that Grandma had worked so far, except for the bean enchiladas, which tasted unlike any enchiladas Emily had ever had before. Grandma's job was going to make her fat.

Christopher took the lid off. "Mmmm. It smells good." He paused. "It looks like chicken and—maybe biscuits?"

"How about dumplings?"

"Yeah, that's what it is." He put the lid back on and came back to the table smiling.

Emily kept sketching.

"I need help deciding on a subject for my newspaper article." Christopher sighed as he sat back down.

"Haven't you figured that out yet?"

He shook his head.

"You'd better choose something—or you won't have enough time to do the interview and then write it."

"I know." He began kicking the chair next to him but at

least he wasn't talking. A minute later he broke Emily's concentration by asking, "When's Grandma getting home?"

Emily shrugged. "Who knows?"

"It's tea day," Christopher said. "I wish I would have gone to help. That was a lot of fun last week. So was the barbecue."

Was he kidding?

"I like it there." Christopher spoke with his mouth full and a cookie crumb shot across the table. Emily shielded her drawing. "Could we go tomorrow? After school?"

Emily shook her head. "I have a lot of homework to do now that I'm a sophomore."

"Please?" he asked. "Sam's not going anymore—but he won't tell me why."

Emily shrugged. She wasn't going to talk about Arielle with Christopher.

"I hate coming home after school." Christopher crossed his arms. "Sam mopes in his room. You're no fun." He paused and then continued. "I feel like Benny in the *Box Car Kids*—but at least his older siblings were nice to him." Christopher pushed back his chair and took his glass to the sink.

Emily felt like she should say something to him—but had no idea what.

"I'm going to go play with Toby." He headed for the back door.

She sighed. "I'll come out in a minute."

It was Grandma being gone. That was what was really wrong. It made everyone out of sorts.

"SORRY I'M LATE!" Grandma's voice rang out from the kitchen.

Emily stirred on the couch, bumping her leg against Christopher, who was sprawled out on the other end. Thankfully *Oprah* had ended and the news was on.

"Anybody home?" Grandma sounded too cheery.

"In here," Emily said, turning off the evening news. Even though it wasn't as inappropriate as daytime TV, Grandma still didn't like Christopher watching it.

Her little brother sat up and yawned. He looked limp from the heat and his late afternoon nap.

"What are you up to?" Grandma stood in the doorway to the family room.

"Taking it easy," Emily said, pulling her knees to her chest.

"Where's Grandpa?"

Emily shrugged. She hadn't seen him all afternoon.

"He's in the shop," Christopher said.

"How about Sam?"

"Up in his room, moping." Emily stood.

"About . . . ?" Grandma looked from Christopher to Emily.

Emily stretched. Was Grandma serious? The whole town knew. How had she missed it?

Emily felt a *duh* look cross her face. "Arielle," she said.

Grandma had one of those blank adult looks on her face. "What happened?"

"Sam insulted her and won't apologize." Emily pulled the hair fastener out of her hair and shook it out.

"Oh." A pained look quickly crossed Grandma's face and then she glanced at her watch. "Well, it's six o'clock. I was expecting that the table would be set."

Emily headed into the kitchen without answering. "Yeah, well, we were expecting a little support around here," she muttered.

"Pardon?" Grandma asked.

Emily turned. Grandma's hearing was better than she thought. "We expected you home sooner."

"Emily." Grandma had that "that's enough" tone in her voice.

Emily began distributing the plates around the table as Grandpa came through the back door. He took his hat from his head and put it on the shelf and then turned toward the kitchen. He looked tired. Emily looked closely as she headed toward the table with four glasses in her hands. His forehead was all scrunched up with more wrinkles than usual.

He turned toward Grandma. "There you are," he said.

She closed the refrigerator door with her foot.

"You're late." Grandpa hooked his thumbs into the straps of his overalls.

"It was tea day." Grandma turned toward him, the full salad bowl in her hands.

Grandpa took a deep breath and then exhaled slowly. "Char," he said, "you're never around. I was thinking this afternoon that if I want to see you, I'm going to have to check into Bedford Gardens."

Emily turned her back to her grandparents, smiling.

Chapter Sixteen

Charlotte stood at Ruth's door, knocking. Red said she'd been feeling under the weather all day.

"Come in," called out a weak voice.

Charlotte entered. Ruth wore a cotton robe and sat on her perfectly made daybed, her legs tucked to the side. She held a book in her hands. "Oh, hello, dear." She put the book on the coffee table and swung her feet to the floor and started to stand.

"Oh, don't get up," Charlotte said. "I just wanted to stop in and say hello." She'd reminded herself not to ask Ruth how she was feeling.

Ruth's eyes sparkled. "Do sit down."

Charlotte sat on the wingback chair. "Do you need anything?"

Ruth smoothed her robe over her lap. "How much time do you have?"

"Well, not much is going on today. No one seems to want to dance without you. A waltz is playing on the sound system, but everyone is sitting down."

"Oh, that Red. Why doesn't he ask one of the other girls to dance?"

"Well, his knee is pretty sore."

Ruth laughed. "Oh, that's right. But he says the same thing every other day I'm not feeling well." Ruth's eyes grew distant.

"So, does he have—as the kids would say—a crush on you?" Charlotte smiled.

Ruth chuckled. "Oh, he might, but I'm much too old for him. And besides, I've never been interested in another relationship, not since my Arnie passed on."

"How long ago was that?"

Ruth sighed. "Thirty-four years ago."

Charlotte's hand went to her throat. "Arnie was much younger than I imagined when he died."

Ruth nodded. "Only sixty-three."

Charlotte wanted to gasp. That was two years younger than she was. "What did he have?" She regretted asking as soon as it came out.

Ruth made eye contact with Charlotte. "He drowned out in Puget Sound. He'd been sailing. He'd been despondent, depressed, but the new doctor he was going to was helping. He was a specialist, a geriatric psychiatrist. Then, just as Arnie was finally getting better, well enough to even sail again, he got caught in a storm, a physical storm." Ruth paused. "There haven't been many times in my life that I've questioned God, but that was one of them."

"I'm sorry," Charlotte said.

Ruth reached over and took her hand. "Thank you, dear. Just love that husband of yours, that farmer of yours." Ruth continued talking, more than she ever had before. She told Charlotte her husband had loved the land too, even more than he loved the sea. He was a geologist and that was why they ended up in places like Montana, Utah, California, and finally Seattle. He loved to golf and sail and hike. Ruth ended up becoming a passable golfer herself, just by spending so much time playing with him. Arnie retired not too long after they moved to Washington.

"And when did you retire?" Charlotte asked.

"Me?" Ruth smiled. "Oh, this is quite the story. I actually un-retired. I never worked as a nurse after I came to the United States, until after Arnie died. I thought I was going to go raving mad, so I went back to school and studied nursing again and then worked in a birthing center."

Charlotte leaned forward. "Ruth, I had no idea."

"It's true. I worked from the time I was sixty-five until I was seventy-seven. Of course I never told anyone how old I was, except my supervisor. They all thought I was in my fifties." She smiled again.

Charlotte clasped her hands together. "Oh, that's wonderful!"

"I thought of that when you first came here," Ruth said. "I thought of all that you could still have ahead of you, but then I met your grandchildren." Ruth paused for a long moment. "They're the most important thing in your future." She looked directly into Charlotte's eyes.

Charlotte tilted her head.

"You are truly blessed."

Charlotte pursed her lips together and then said, "Thank you, Ruth. You know, I've been regretting lately that I didn't become a nurse years ago, like I intended . . . that I haven't had a career."

There. After thinking it for the last week, she'd finally said it.

"I would imagine," Ruth said, "that you've been doing all the things a nurse does for all these years. Putting on Band-Aids, listening, triaging, counseling, administering first aid, consulting with the doctor. All of that." The old woman reached her wrinkled hand out to Charlotte. "Don't underestimate all you've done. And certainly don't underestimate what you're doing now—and I don't mean helping out temporarily here."

Charlotte knew exactly what she meant. She'd needed the reminder. She hadn't had time at all for Madison and Jennifer at the barbecue, and Sam, Emily, Christopher—and Bob—had been demanding and moody the night before. She thought it was good for them to have her busy temporarily, but she couldn't see it being a good thing for the long run.

"And, you know," Ruth said, "those kids need you."

Charlotte raised her eyebrows.

"Of course, they know their mother died, that she didn't choose to leave them, but emotionally it can feel like abandonment, and they could have scars."

Charlotte nodded. She'd read that before, soon after Denise died.

"People who have been abandoned are more likely to develop addictions, and they have a harder time developing meaningful relationships."

"Really?" Charlotte hadn't read that.

"I know from my own experience," Ruth said. "You see, both Arnie and I were abandoned as children. Funny how we choose each other, isn't it? My mother died when I was a child, and my father sent me off to boarding school. Sure, he would take me to the symphony or to a soccer match now and then, but that was all. And then he remarried when I was seventeen and had an entirely new family, which I never felt welcomed into." Her eyes grew moist. "And poor Arnie. Both his parents died, and he was raised by his indifferent grandmother. And then, on top of that devastating experience, he had all the horrors of the war."

Charlotte winced.

"So you see, dear, raising your grandchildren, loving your grandchildren, is the most important thing you can do right now. With your support and God's intervention, they can heal." She sighed again. "They are so fortunate to have you and be young in a time when more thought is put toward children and their needs."

Charlotte agreed. "Thank you," she said sincerely. She *was* fortunate to have her family, all of them. "Ruth," she said, leaning forward, "do you have relatives in England still? That you keep in touch with?"

"Well." The older woman sat up a little straighter. "Funny you should ask. I just received a letter this week from one of my great-nephews. His father passed on two years ago, and his son has been settling his affairs. Now this nephew and I are e-mailing each other. Arielle set up a Yahoo account for me." Her eyes twinkled. "It's been most delightful. He has a son—my great-grand-nephew. A darling little four-year-old. And a brand-new baby girl." She paused for a moment. "We'll see where that goes, but for now, for the first time in thirty-four years, I have family again."

Charlotte relished Ruth's good news and then glanced at her watch. "Oh, my. I'd better go see if I can get the others dancing."

"Good idea," Ruth said. She stood slowly. "Now, just to let you know, Dr. Carr is stopping by in about half an hour. Please tell the other residents it's just a routine checkup. You know how alarmed everyone gets, and I most definitely do not want to be in the middle of the Bedford Gardens gossip mill."

Charlotte didn't believe Ruth that it was a routine checkup, not if Dr. Carr was coming to her, but she didn't want to pry. "I'll discourage any drama," Charlotte said. Boy, there were times when the nursing home and high school seemed a lot alike.

CHARLOTTE TURNED THE MUSIC OFF after Dr. Carr arrived. None of the residents wanted to dance or even visit.

"The doctor has never come here to see her," Red said.

Charlotte reassured him that it was a routine checkup.

"I don't believe you," he replied.

Arielle's arrival didn't change Red's mood. He refused to check his mailbox to see if his insurance company had responded to his written claim, and he didn't want to play another game of baseball on the Wii.

"How about a craft?" Arielle suggested to Charlotte. "I can get out the scrapbooking supplies."

The idea sounded as good as any. Stephanie had started the residents on scrapbooking, making pages and cards.

Most of them had photos they had left down in the craft closet to work with. As they set up the supplies, Charlotte asked Arielle how school was, how her classes were going, and how her college search was panning out. Arielle answered sweetly to each question.

"How are things going with Sam?" Charlotte finally asked as she set out sheets of paper on the craft table.

"Fine," Arielle answered and hurried back toward the supply closet for the paints. Obviously she didn't want to talk about anything important to Charlotte. She shouldn't have asked—it wasn't her business anyway.

Dr. Carr began walking down the open staircase. Red struggled to stand, leaning against his cane as he lifted himself out of an overstuffed chair. "How is she, Doc?"

Dr. Carr smiled. "Ask her in a minute. She said she's had enough of being in her room. She'll be down shortly."

"Well then," Red said, leaning against his cane, a smile on his face. "Maybe we should dance after all."

Dr. Carr nodded at Charlotte. "Actually, what you have set up looks like a good activity for today."

Red tottered over to the table and sat down. When Betty tried to sit beside him, he politely said that place was saved as he busied himself with his envelope of photos.

Just as Ruth started down the staircase, dressed in her usual linen skirt, pressed blouse, and practical shoes, a car backfired in the parking lot.

"That sounds like Sam," Charlotte said.

Arielle blushed and the front door flew open as Christopher rushed in. "Grandma," he blurted out, "is it okay if I help today?"

"Of course," she said.

Christopher ran back out and a minute later Emily shuffled in after him. The car backfired again.

"Where's Sam going?" Charlotte asked.

Christopher shrugged, dropped his backpack on a chair, and then sat next to Betty. "He said he had to go back to school—he forgot something."

Meanwhile, Ruth settled in next to Red. He patted her hand, and she smiled at him. Charlotte's heart jumped. Poor Red. He really had it bad for Ruth.

"Come sit," Ruth said to Emily, motioning to the chair next to her.

"We had to come here to see Grandma," Emily said quietly, fingering a piece of floral paper. Charlotte ignored her. She had given Emily her undivided attention yesterday evening, but Emily would not cooperate. She complained and complained and wouldn't focus on an idea for her art project.

"Oh, you poor thing," Ruth said. "What do you need?"

Emily slumped against the table, her arms folded in front of her. "I have to do a service project in art. Can you imagine? It's a sort of beautify-your-world project." She sighed. "I was supposed to tell Ms. Carey my idea today—but I can't think of anything."

A smile threatened to cross Ruth's face. "Does it have to be your world? Or could it be someone else's?"

"Like a church. That's what Ashley's doing. Or a park."

"Or a nursing home?"

Emily nodded. "Yeah, that was on the list."

Ruth looked around the lobby. "Well, what do you think?"

"What do I think? That it would take *Extreme Makeover* to beautify this place."

Ruth laughed. "Oh, yes. *Extreme Makeover*. I've watched that show before—and cried. Well," she said, "I don't think they have an *Extreme Makeover, Nursing Home Edition* show though."

"My point exactly," Emily said.

Charlotte felt embarrassed at her granddaughter's tone and moved down the table to help Aggie fix a sticker onto a card she was making, all the while still concentrating on Emily and Ruth's conversation.

"There are lots of ways to bring beauty into a place. For example, the bucket of flowers your grandmother gave us brought lots of beauty."

Emily groaned. "This is supposed to be something lasting. Something permanent."

"Oh, dear," Ruth said, as if the problem were unsolvable. She turned her attention to Red's scrapbooking page. There were three photos of him playing baseball. "Oh, my. Look at you, Red."

He smiled.

Emily buried her face in her arms.

"You know what would be wonderful," Ruth said to Charlotte, not waiting for an answer, "is if we had photos of ourselves around here, not just in a scrapbook or in our rooms. Say, out in the halls, by our doors."

"That's a great idea," Charlotte said.

Emily's head stayed down.

"I think it would really brighten things up around here," Ruth said. "What do you think, Red?"

He glanced at Emily. Her head turned a little, as if she was listening. "We could make mats for the photos from the scrapbooking paper. But what would we do for frames?"

"Well, I wonder." Ruth held her pencil in midair.

Emily's head lifted, just a little.

"Emily, dear," Ruth said. "Could you coordinate the project? For your art requirement?"

"Maybe." Emily sat up. "I could talk with Ms. Carey." Then she slumped a little again. "But what about the frames? They're expensive."

Ruth tapped her chin. "Let's give that some more thought. Why don't we make a standard-size mat and go from there?"

"Maybe Uncle Pete can make the frames," Emily said.

Charlotte stepped forward. "He's pretty busy right now, Em, with harvest starting up again." She didn't want Pete distracted from his work. That would only put more stress on Bob, and her having a job seemed to be all the stress he could handle at the moment.

Christopher blinked several times, as if he was trying to figure out how to phrase something he wanted to say. "Miss Ruth," he finally said. He'd probably forgotten that her last name was Blake. "I need an idea too. For my newspaper article."

"Well," Ruth said, obviously pleased to be consulted, "what is your new favorite thing? What are you most interested in?"

Christopher took a deep breath. "That's the problem. I'm interested in lots of things." He dug in his pants pocket and pulled out a tattered piece of paper. "I was interested in a manure pile in Monroe County." He glanced at Charlotte. "But I took that off the list."

He held the list up to his face. "I was thinking about writing about the football team or why there isn't soccer in Bedford or about the school lunch program."

"Those all sound like good ideas," Ruth said.

Christopher frowned.

"But they don't really hold your interest?"

He nodded.

"Well, what really interests you right now?"

Christopher twisted his nose and mouth around for a moment and then his face broke out into a grin. "I know!" He nearly leaped off his chair. "Coming here."

"Well, then," Ruth said. "Write about here."

"But what about here? There's so much." He slumped back onto his chair.

Charlotte helped Betty run a piece of paper through the portable paper cutter and then patted Christopher's shoulder.

"Well, start a new list. A Bedford Gardens list," Ruth suggested.

A moment later Charlotte asked Emily if Sam was coming back to get her and Christopher, but what she really wanted to know was if he planned to give Arielle a ride home.

"He said he'd see us back at the farm," Emily answered.

Charlotte wondered what was up with him. "Arielle, do you need a ride home?"

"No thanks, Mrs. Stevenson," she answered. "My dad will pick me up. He'll be here any minute."

CHARLOTTE SURVEYED THE CARDS and scrapbooking pages. Aggie had made a birthday card for her niece Sally, Ruth had made a blank card to send to her nephew, and Betty had taken a card and affixed a photo of herself, circa 1955, showing her wearing a wide-legged pants suit and holding a bowling ball in her hands, standing at the top of a bowling lane.

"Can we go?" Emily asked. "I want to check with Pete about making frames."

"I need to check on Ruth first," Charlotte said. "And please don't talk with Pete until we've had a chance to explore other ideas." She turned and started up the stairs. After she'd finished her card, Ruth had asked Diane to request that the cook send a tray up to her room for dinner, saying she was feeling a little weak.

Christopher sat on the second level with Red, helping him with the jigsaw puzzle. "You know what would be better than a photo of them now?" Charlotte could tell that Emily was on a roll as she marched alongside her grandmother. "An old photo. From their prime."

"Emily," Charlotte pleaded.

"No, seriously. Aren't you just dying to know how everyone looked when they were young? What they wore? All of that?"

Charlotte shook her head. She could imagine what most of them looked like—she was old enough to know what they wore. But Emily wasn't. Still, it was a good idea. "Now go wait with Christopher," Charlotte said. "I'll be right back."

She knocked softly on Ruth's door and again heard a faint, "Come in."

This time Ruth lay back on her daybed, still in her skirt and blouse, with her eyes closed. "Is that you, Charlotte?"

"Yes. I just wanted to check on you before I left."

"Thank you. I'm fine. Just tired."

"Do you need anything?"

"No, deary, but thank you."

Charlotte said good-bye and turned to leave.

Ruth called out softly, "Actually, there's one thing." She opened her eyes. "Charlotte, do you think it's possible for a person to go home again?"

"Well . . ." That was hard for Charlotte to answer. Bedford had always been her home. "Are you talking about going back to London?"

Ruth smiled. "Maybe," she said.

"Would it feel like home? After all this time?" Charlotte couldn't even imagine how much London had changed in seventy-plus years.

Ruth nodded. "I see what you mean."

"But I suppose there would only be one way to know for sure." Charlotte smiled at her friend. "Are you planning on a trip to London?"

"Oh, dear," Ruth answered. "I'm just dreaming, that's all. Mum's the word, please. I don't want any talk going around."

Charlotte agreed. As she started through the doorway, Ruth called out again, "Would you mind if Lillian and Stephanie join us next Wednesday for tea?"

"That would be lovely," Charlotte said.

"Even though it's more work?"

"That's fine." Charlotte paused. "Ruth, I'm wondering if

having Sam and Arielle over Saturday morning will be too much for you."

"Oh, I'm much better in the morning." She sat up. "In fact, that's when we should be dancing. No, please. I'm so looking forward to having Sam and Arielle join me. I'm excited to hear what Sam has found out about colleges."

So am I, Charlotte thought as she said good-bye and closed the door.

A minute later Charlotte patted Red on the shoulder, and then Emily and Christopher followed her down the staircase and they headed home.

Chapter Seventeen

On Friday morning before school started, Sam knocked on Mr. Santos's office door. The counselor had gone home early the day before, even though Sam had an appointment with him to talk about colleges. Sam had hurried back after dropping off Christopher and Emily at the nursing home and was two minutes late for his appointment, but Mr. Santos hadn't waited. How could Mr. Santos be so thoughtless? Teachers, especially counselors, weren't supposed to miss appointments.

Sam knocked again and then pressed his nose against the frosted-glass window. He couldn't hear anything and it didn't seem like the light was on either.

"He's not coming in today." Arielle stood behind him. "He's ill."

"How do you know?" Sam tried the doorknob.

"I was just in the office when he called in. He has strep throat." Arielle slipped a note under the door. "You can leave a note this way—or one in the office."

Sam groaned. "Will he be back by this afternoon?"

Arielle crossed her arms. "What do you think, Sam?" She turned on her heels and headed down the hall.

Was strep throat that bad? Sam slapped his hand against the frosted glass and then jerked it back as the glass shook. That was all he needed—a destruction of property rap. He'd made Arielle mad, really mad, obviously, and now he wasn't going to get to try out for the soccer team, unless Mr. Santos got better, pronto. He shuffled down the hall toward English to sit by himself, again.

AFTER SCHOOL, Sam headed out to his car. Mr. Santos hadn't come back, and by lunchtime there was a rumor going around that he had scarlet fever and wouldn't be back for a week. Scarlet fever? Who got scarlet fever anymore?

"Sam!" He turned around, slowly. Arielle was hurrying toward him. She hadn't talked with him all day. "Can I get a ride to the nursing home? My dad is out on a call."

"Sure." He tried to smile. "I need to wait for Emily and Christopher though."

They climbed into the car, and Sam rolled down both windows and then they sat silently for a minute. Then it dawned on him that she usually went to the nursing home for seventh period. "Hey, aren't you late?"

She nodded. "I made some phone calls from the school about colleges."

"Really?" Sam was surprised that was allowed at school.

"Mr. Duncan gave me permission. He let me into Mr. Santos's office—he'd left a list of phone numbers for me."

Sam shifted in his seat. He really needed to say something,

explain why he'd acted the way he had, said what he did on Monday. "Um, Arielle—"

"Shotgun!" Christopher called out.

"No, you don't!" Emily's voice pierced Sam like a dentist drill.

He opened the car door and stepped out. "Actually, you both get the back seat. I'm giving Arielle a ride."

"Oh," Emily answered, raising her eyebrows.

Sam shook his head. She'd better not say anything.

The drive to the nursing home seemed to take an eternity. Arielle stared straight ahead, her hands in her lap. She wore a blue-striped blouse that made her eyes extra noticeable, her hair was twisted on top of her head, and she wore big gold-hoop earrings.

"Do you work today?" Emily asked.

Arielle turned in her seat, a smile on her face. "No. But I work tomorrow, from nine to six."

Sam concentrated on stopping fully at the intersection of Lincoln and Main, and tuned out the conversation about magazines and fashion. Christopher let out a big yawn, and a second later Sam was yawning too.

"Tired?" Arielle asked.

Sam shook his head.

"Bored?"

"No." He choked on the word. Did she think he was the biggest jerk there was? "No," he said again. "Not at all." He tried to smile, but it felt like a grimace.

He turned into the parking lot of the nursing home. "Are you going to the football game tonight?" he asked. It was a home game, the first one of the season.

"I think so. With Halley."

"Oh." Sam pulled into a parking space, wondering whether, if he had played football this year like he did last year, that would have impressed Arielle.

"Thanks for the ride." She opened the car door.

Sam opened his and ran around to her side, holding the door and then slamming it shut after she'd climbed out. "Can I talk to you?" he asked.

"Sure."

They started toward the nursing home, away from the car.

"Are you mad at me?" he asked.

She swung her bag over her shoulder and shrugged.

"I didn't mean what I said on Monday. I did have a good time."

"I know," she answered. "But it was like you cared more about what Jake thought than how I felt."

Whoa. How did girls come up with statements like that? Sam wanted to smack his head, to try to dislodge—

"Thanks for the ride," she said as they reached the door.

He hurried to open it. "I'm trying—"

"What time will you pick me up in the morning?"

Did she still want to go? "Um," he said.

"Ruth said the game starts at seven. How about six fifty?" Arielle asked.

"Okay," Sam said, and then before the door swung shut, he added, "I might see you at the game tonight."

Arielle shrugged again. "I promised Halley I'd sit by her."

On the way back to the car, he decided not to go to the game after all. What was the point?

FOR JUST A MINUTE, Sam considered sleeping through his alarm on Saturday morning. What if he didn't show? What would Arielle think of that? His eyes flew open. He could pretty much guess what she would think of that. If she was upset over a stupid comment, what would she be like over a premeditated action? Well, sleeping in didn't have to be premeditated. He could just say it was an accident, that he forgot to set his alarm, or slept through it or something.

He yawned and stretched his arms. It was five forty-five. Earlier than he had to get up for school. There was something wrong with this. He still didn't get it. He couldn't understand Ruth being such a dedicated fan. Aunt Rosemary was the most fanatical sportswoman he knew. Would she get up at the crack of dawn for a Huskers game?

He swung his feet onto the floor. Probably. Maybe Ruth wasn't that weird after all. And he liked her accent. He just thought it was a little strange that she would ask him and Arielle to her apartment at such an odd hour of the day, even to watch a soccer match.

He hoped Arielle wouldn't want to talk more about Monday. What had she said? That he cared more about what Jake thought than how she felt? Well, it wasn't like he'd planned to. He'd been caught off guard.

He showered, dressed, and tiptoed down the stairs. He didn't need to. The kitchen light was on, and Grandma and Grandpa were both sitting at the table with their coffee. Grandpa was reading out loud from his Bible.

Sam cleared his throat and Grandma turned and smiled, and then put her hand on Grandpa's arm and said, "Bob."

Grandpa turned too and said good morning.

"I made cinnamon rolls for you to take." Grandma stood, her coffee cup in her hand. "They're on the counter."

Was that weird? Sam wondered. For him to take food? Would Arielle think that was cool? Or jerkish? "Thanks, Grandma," he said.

"And, Sam," Grandma said as he lifted the pan of rolls from the counter. "Would you be attentive to Ruth's needs? She hasn't been feeling well. If she seems really tired or acts strangely, please let the receptionist know immediately."

Yikes. What was Grandma trying to tell him? "Is everything okay—you know, with Ruth?" Was she going to pass out or something? Because he didn't want to have to try to do CPR on an old person.

"She'll be just fine. I just don't want you to hesitate to get help." She patted his shoulder. "Have fun. And tell Ruth and Arielle hello."

He nodded, but he probably wouldn't tell either one.

Arielle was standing on her porch when he pulled into her driveway; she hurried toward the car before it had even stopped. She had a sweatshirt tied around her waist and wore jeans and a T-shirt. There was actually a bit of a chill in the air. Maybe summer wouldn't last forever.

"Yum!" she said as she sat down and began fastening her seat belt. "Something smells great. Cinnamon rolls, right?"

Sam nodded.

"What a good idea to bring something."

Sam smiled. "Grandma made them."

They rode silently. Sam tried to think of something to talk about. It was as if all of his thoughts and ideas were swimming underwater in a murky pond and couldn't quite get to the surface, but he wanted to say something—something that would make Arielle feel better about him.

"The sunrise is pretty." Arielle's face was turned away from him, toward her window.

Sam glanced over to the right. It *was* pretty. Oranges and pinks and reds melded together and rose over the sloping hills to the east of Bedford.

"That would be fun to watercolor. Your grandma said that would be a good project to do at the nursing home."

Sam groaned.

"What's wrong?"

Was he acting like a jerk again? "Oh, it's nothing," he said. "Just that Emily recruited Pete to make frames for the residents and he asked me to help this afternoon."

"That sounds like fun too."

He almost asked if she wanted to help but then he remembered that she had to work at nine. That would turn out nicely. They'd have to leave Ruth's as soon as the match was over.

They tried the door of the nursing home, but it was locked. They knocked but no one came.

"Do you have your cell?" Arielle asked. "You could call your Grandma and ask her to call whoever is in charge here this morning."

Sam handed her the cinnamon rolls and began digging his phone out of his pants pocket just as the door swung open.

"There you are," Ruth said. "I was just about to call your grandmother to see when you'd left." She was totally dressed—a skirt, blouse, necklace, and even lipstick. She didn't look she was going to watch a soccer match. "Come on, come on," she said. "The match starts in five minutes."

Ruth led the way up the staircase, taking them quickly. She didn't look sick, not at all. He'd never seen her take the elevator. She turned to the left at the top of the stairs and made funny circular motions with her hand. "Can't miss the kickoff," she said. "Come along."

She opened the door of her apartment. A big-screen TV sat inside a cabinet with doors that were slid open. A sort of couch-like bed with pillows lining the back was pulled toward the center of the room and a wingback chair was beside it. "You two take the sofa," she instructed, pulling a scarf from the back of the chair. "And I'll sit here." She arranged the scarf around her neck and sat. Sam snuck a closer look. It was a knit scarf with a lion, the Chelsea lion. The design looked really old; the blue of the scarf was faded.

"Ready?" Ruth asked, her eyes sparkling. She nodded toward the TV. "The lads are."

Arielle placed the pan of rolls on the table and sat down beside Sam. The Chelsea players, wearing blue uniforms, and the Manchester United players, wearing white, ran onto the field. The referee blew his whistle and the match began with Man U taking possession. The picture on the TV was better than any Sam had ever seen. Ruth probably had the best TV in Bedford. The center forward for Man U dribbled toward the Chelsea goal, passing to the Man U wing.

"Drat!" Ruth called out. "Stop him!" Then she began to clap. A Chelsea defender cleared the ball, sending it high into the air, clear to the midway line, and a Chelsea midfielder dropped it to the ground and passed it forward. "Splendid!" Ruth yelled.

Sam grinned at Arielle, and she smiled back at him.

The hordes of fans sang and chanted, adding a lyrical soundtrack to the game. A Chelsea midfielder passed to a forward, and back and forth the ball went, the players working together to move the game forward and open up a chance for a goal. It was the way his coach in San Diego had been trying to get Sam's old team to play.

It was obvious that the players shared a team camaraderie, a passion. Sam missed that. It was the thrill of running as hard as you could, reaching the ball, and setting up a play. There was nothing like it.

As the first half ended at the forty-fifth-minute mark, Ruth was on her feet. "Well, one-one is a fine place to be. We'll take them in the second half." She took off her scarf and folded it over the back of her chair. "Now, let's talk breakfast. Come along," she said, starting into the kitchen but stopping at the table.

"Did you bring this?" she asked Arielle, opening the lid of the cinnamon roll pan.

"No. Sam did."

"Grandma made them," Sam said. Was she upset? Had he intruded on her plan?

"Well, well. God does provide, doesn't He? That's just what we needed." She turned on the kettle and then opened the oven door and pulled out a dish. "We'll have breakfast casserole and rolls," she said. "And tea. In the old days I would have had kippers and tomatoes. But this is much better." Her eyes twinkled.

"Did you make the casserole this morning?" Arielle asked.

"Of course," Ruth said.

"What time did you get up?"

"Oh, you'll see someday. It's hard to sleep when you're old." Ruth smiled.

As she poured the water into the teapot, she asked Sam to check how much time was left until the second half started.

He stood in front of the TV while Arielle put three plates on the table.

"You'd better add a fourth setting," Ruth said.

The clock showed four more minutes left before the second half and Sam announced the time just as there was a knock on the door.

"Would you get that, please, Sam?" Ruth asked. "It's Red."

"Oh, how nice that you invited him too," Arielle said.

Ruth shook her head. "Oh, I didn't invite him," Ruth said. "He just shows up."

Sam opened the door. Red seemed surprised to see him, but came right in. "Oh, and Arielle's here too. Ruth, you've been holding out on me. Why didn't you tell me we had company?"

Ruth ignored him. "Everyone, gather around. We have just enough time for a blessing and then to fill our plates." She prayed a simple and fast prayer and then asked Arielle to get her food first. The game had started as Sam and Red sat on either side of Arielle on the sofa, all of them balancing their plates on their laps.

"I know it's a barbaric way to eat," Ruth said, sitting in the chair. "I only allow it if Chelsea is playing, believe me."

Chelsea scored in the fifty-fifth minute. Luckily, Ruth had finished eating and didn't have her teacup in her hand because she sprang to her feet and did a little jig in the middle of the room. She sat down, laughing. "Did I happen to mention," she gasped, "that Red is a huge Man U fan?"

"I wouldn't say huge," Red said. He took a sip of tea. "I saw them play once when I was in England."

"Still." Ruth clapped her hands together. "Look what my Chelsea has done."

The four of them sat and watched the rest of the game, chatting and enjoying each other's company. With two minutes left in the game, a defender passed to Chelsea midfielder Frank Lampard. A Man U defender slipped on the pitch, and Lampard got around him and took the shot instead of passing.

"Yes!" Ruth shouted as the ball flew to the back of the net, jumping to her feet again and high-fiving Sam and Arielle and then Red, who by now was laughing.

She tugged on either end of her scarf again, did another little jig, and plopped back in her chair. "Now finish strong," she said to the TV. "Don't let your guard down."

Chelsea did finish strong, and as the buzzer sounded, the players swarmed Lampard with unabashed joy. Sam's heart skipped as he watched. That's what he wanted again. To play soccer. He had to try out for the Harding team.

"Thank you, thank you," Ruth said, leaning back in her chair, "for joining me."

Suddenly, Sam felt bad for having an escape plan. "I need to take Arielle to work, but I'll come back and help you clean up," he said.

"I wouldn't hear of it," Ruth said, standing. "In fact I'm going to rest and then I'll clean up. Red will help if I need it, won't you, Red?"

"Of course," he answered.

"Oh dear, Sam. I did want to hear about your plans for your soccer team. Have you done what you needed to do to try out?"

He blushed. "I'm working on it." Why did the whole town, at least the whole nursing home, have to know his business?

"Well," Ruth said. "Please give me an update next week. You know how much I'd like to see you play."

Sam said he would and slid the lid to the cinnamon roll pan into place. He and Arielle said their thank-yous and good-byes and left. As they descended the stairs, Arielle asked if Sam had had fun.

"Yep," he answered.

"Honestly?" she asked.

"Yeah," he said. "It was a lot of fun." What was she getting at? Was she going to start acting weird again? He was so confused.

Chapter Eighteen

Emily pushed open the door of Uncle Pete's truck. "I'll come over to the lumberyard in a minute," she said.

"Hurry." Pete scowled under the bill of his baseball cap. "I need to get back out to the farm."

She slammed the door. Pete had been awfully uptight lately. Sam had said he'd help with the frames, so she wasn't sure what the big deal was. Making thirty frames couldn't be that hard, she thought as she pushed through the door of Fabrics and Fun. She looked around for a minute but the place appeared vacant. Where was Aunt Rosemary? Emily walked out the door and back in several times, dinging the bell over and over.

"I'm coming, I'm coming!" Aunt Rosemary emerged from the back of the store, wiping her hands on her apron. "Oh, Emily. It's you. You little rascal. I thought there was a busload of people out here." Her eyes were wide. "I was playing around with some new craft paints. Want to come see?"

Emily didn't really want to, but she was sure it would hurt Aunt Rosemary's feelings if she protested. "Sure," she said.

"This stuff is kind of cool. All-purpose-like. You can use it on metal or wood. And it washes up really well. Even little kids can use it."

"Even old people?" Emily asked.

Aunt Rosemary chuckled, deep and throaty. "Like me?"

"No." Emily smiled. "You're not old. I meant like the people at Bedford Gardens."

Aunt Rosemary stopped at the worktable in the back. "Oh, I heard about your idea. If the residents can scrapbook like your grandmother says they can, I'm sure this would be a simple little exercise for them." Aunt Rosemary held up a metal can she'd painted a sunflower on. "Isn't that sweet?"

Emily agreed. "So it works on wood—like on a picture frame?"

"Sure, wood, metal, either one."

Emily frowned. "Well, Pete says he'll make some, and Sam said he would help, but so far nothing has been done."

"What about your grandfather? Can't he help out?"

Emily picked up the bottle of paint. "I doubt it. He's been really grumpy, ever since Grandma started working at the nursing home. He says he's going to have to become a resident there if he ever wants to see her again."

Aunt Rosemary chuckled as she placed the can back on the table. "Well, it doesn't hurt to ask."

"I don't think I could afford this paint anyway." Emily sighed. The project was turning out to be a real pain.

"Well, I could donate a set of paints. For the cause," Aunt Rosemary said.

"Really?"

"Sure. Every once in a while I like to do something community-minded—this sounds like as good a project as any." She patted Emily's shoulder. "It's a fine idea, putting up photos of the residents from when they were young. You know that's how they still think of themselves—as young."

Emily wrinkled her nose.

"I know I do. I scare myself when I look in the mirror. I feel like I'm thirty on the inside—and then I wonder who that gray-haired, wrinkly old lady is staring back at me." Aunt Rosemary threw back her head and laughed.

Emily tried to smile but she couldn't figure out what was so funny. When Rosemary stopped, Emily said, "Well, thank you for offering to donate the paint."

"You bet." Aunt Rosemary followed Emily back through the store. "Hey, who brought you in to town?"

"Pete. He's over at the lumberyard trying to find scrap wood for the frames. In fact, I'd better get over there to meet him."

"Keep me updated," Aunt Rosemary said, giving Emily a hug at the door. "I'm proud of you for helping out at Bedford Gardens—there's nothing like service to others in this life to make us grow."

Emily thanked her and walked down the sidewalk. It wasn't like she'd decided to do the frames on her own or anything. She was being forced to do this. Didn't everyone get that?

The afternoon heat was sweltering. She ducked into the pharmacy and headed toward the magazine rack.

"Hi, Emily." Arielle stood behind the counter wearing her white smock. She looked a little tired.

"Has the new *Vogue* come in?"

"Nope. I checked."

"Oh." Emily turned around.

"What are you up to today?" Arielle asked. "Riding the horses?"

"Nah," Emily answered. "I'm trying to figure out my art service project."

"Oh, that's right. The frames."

"Yeah. Uncle Pete is helping me. In fact, I'd better get over to the lumberyard." As she headed toward the door, the back of a frame in the window display caught her attention. It was metal. "Oh, look at that."

"We have boxes of those. Apparently there was a mixup in an order a couple of months ago and then the distributor went out of business so we got stuck with them."

"How many do you have altogether?" Emily asked.

"Oh, four boxes at least. So, maybe forty." Arielle pulled the frame out of the window display and handed it to Emily.

She turned it over in her hands. The edges were all smooth, they could be painted, and they would hang neatly on the wall. And each one cost eight dollars.

"Hey, does Mr. Kepler ever make donations? You know, for charity?" Emily asked, handing the frame back to Arielle.

"I don't know." Arielle slipped it back into the display window. "Why?"

"I THINK I SHOULD ASK Mr. Kepler about the frames," Emily said to Uncle Pete. "Maybe he would donate them."

"I think I should buy the wood," Uncle Pete said. "If he

won't donate the frames, then we're out of luck. I can't come back on Monday to get the wood."

Emily must have looked awfully hurt because Uncle Pete said, nicely, "Look, little lady, let's get the wood. If we don't need it for the frames we can return it and get our money back. Okay?"

"Okay." Emily took her wallet out of her purse. She hoped she had enough money left to buy another magazine.

"I'll get it," Pete said. "Think of it as my contribution to your endeavors to make Bedford Gardens a more tolerable place." He pulled his gloves out of his other back pocket, slipped them on his hands, and then gathered up a pile of long pieces of wood.

"Thanks," she muttered, slipping her wallet back into her purse. Maybe the magazine would be in by Monday when she talked to Mr. Kepler.

SUNDAY EVENING before youth group, Emily turned around slowly in the basement of the church. Something was different. It was the same old carpet. The same old mint green walls. The same old pillars holding up the same old church. What was different?

The signs. Ashley had completed her project. The words were painted in rich jewel tones and perfectly scripted. NURSERY. TODDLERS. PRESCHOOL CLASS. KINDERGARTEN—SECOND GRADE. THIRD—SIXTH GRADE. JUNIOR HIGH. HIGH SCHOOL. A wave of jealousy swept over Emily. Ashley was already done with her project, and Emily hadn't even started. Ms. Carey was going to be so impressed.

"Oh, hi, Em." Ashley approached with a digital camera in her hand.

"Nice work," Emily said. "Your signs are really cool." Could Ashley detect her resentment? Emily tried to smile.

"Thanks. It came together really quickly. I painted them Friday night and sealed them last night."

"Oh. So, it really didn't take much time?"

"I wouldn't say that. I stayed up half the night on Friday. You know. This stuff always takes longer than you think."

Emily nodded.

"I'm just going to take a photo of each one before everyone gets here."

"Okay," Emily said. Wasn't that just like Ashley? Not wanting to draw attention to herself?

What would Emily do if Mr. Kepler wouldn't donate the frames? Uncle Pete was right—Grandpa wasn't interested in cutting sheet metal, that was for sure. She'd broached the subject during dinner, and he shot it down in half a second. "That Rosemary," he had said. "She thinks I have all the time in the world. I don't have an empty house like—"

"Bob," Grandma had said, cutting him off.

Emily walked to the room where they met for youth group. The HIGH SCHOOL sign had people's faces painted in the two O's of SCHOOL. Emily peered closely. The faces were of two girls, and one had red hair, bright red, and the other had blonde—well, yellow, actually. Emily smiled as she pushed open the door of the classroom and sat down on the metal chair next to the couch, where Sam sat next to Jake. When did Jake start coming to youth group? Arielle sat on the other side of the room.

"I heard you were doing a service project at Bedford Gardens," Jason, the youth pastor, said.

Emily blushed. Arielle must have said something.

"That's really cool. Sometimes older people in our society are forgotten, especially in a nursing home. You're doing a good thing."

Emily could feel the heat in her face. If everyone knew how she really felt about the nursing home, they wouldn't be praising her left and right. It was getting awkward. "Did everyone notice Ashley's new signs?"

"No," Jason said.

"I did," Arielle said.

Desperate to get the attention off herself, Emily suggested that everyone go out to the fellowship hall and see what Ashley had done. Jason led the way and the entire group filed out.

Ashley looked mortified when she realized what they were doing, and she gave Emily a searching look.

Emily shrugged and smiled, but felt like she'd just betrayed her friend.

"Your signs are great," Arielle said.

Sam stood back.

"Yeah." Jake spun around, looking from sign to sign. Then he said, "But I hope we won't have to go to the nursing home next week to look at Emily's project."

Sam was nodding in agreement for a moment—until Arielle said, "Why Jake?" And then, "Why Sam?"

Emily smiled and stole a look at Sam as a frown spread across his face. Sam couldn't seem to keep himself out of the doghouse.

Ashley slipped into the high school room and the rest of the class followed.

After singing a few songs, Jason opened his Bible and read, "'Trust in the Lord with all your heart and lean not on your own understanding; in all your ways submit to him, and he will make your paths straight.'

"That's from Proverbs," he said, closing his Bible. "It's one of my favorite passages." He sat back on the stool. "Tonight I want to talk about what it means to trust God." He looked around the room, smiling at each student. "Do any of you have an example of a time when you really trusted God?"

No one answered. "Come on, you guys," he said.

Emily yawned.

"How about an example of a time when you didn't trust God?" Jason asked.

Arielle raised her hand, just a little. "I kind of have an example, actually of both not trusting and then trusting. There was a time, a few years ago, when I really wanted to move away from Bedford, even though I've lived here my entire life. I was in junior high and felt really out of place. Finally I prayed about it, begged God to find my dad a job somewhere else so we could move. But He didn't answer my prayer. Finally I figured out that He had—that He wanted us to stay. So then I started praying every day, asking Him to help me like living in Bedford, to help me reach out to my classmates. And to trust Him."

Emily took a deep breath. She had no idea that Arielle was so spiritual. She stole another look at Sam. He was staring at his hands.

Jason encouraged the kids to think about something

they were struggling with right now and ask God to help them with it, to see how He would provide. Or wouldn't provide, Emily thought, thinking of Arielle's story. She sighed. Why did this art project have her in such a funk?

She tried to pray. *Dear God,* she started, *please make Mr. Kepler give me the frames.* That didn't sound right. *Please help me finish the project.* That wasn't right either. What was it she needed to pray? *Please help me do something to help the people at the nursing home.* Was that it? Was that what she really needed help with? *Please help me want to help the people in the nursing home.* And then she added, *And please show me how to trust You.*

MONDAY AFTER SCHOOL, Sam gave Emily a ride to the pharmacy.

"Thanks for waiting," Emily said as she opened the car door.

"Who said I was waiting?"

"Sam," she pleaded, "how am I going to get home?"

"Walk to the nursing home. Grandma will give you a ride."

"But it's so hot. And now it's muggy too. Why don't you and Christopher come in? I'm just going to ask Mr. Kepler about the frames."

"Nah," Sam said.

"I want to go home," Christopher said. "I need to work on my interview questions."

"Come on, you guys," Emily pleaded again. Christopher could have worked on his questions all weekend, and Sam was just being a creep. It was because of Arielle; she sat with her friends again at lunch and her dad gave her a ride this afternoon.

"Emily, get out of the car," Sam said. "You have your cell. Call Grandma and ask her to pick you up here."

"But that means I'd have to wait for an hour, at least. You know how long it takes her to get out of there."

Sam shrugged.

"Let's go," Christopher said. "Or I'm going to forget my ideas."

Emily climbed out of the car. She really didn't want to go to the nursing home today. She couldn't believe how much time she spent there, especially as someone who hated the place. She slammed the car door. Sam was ridiculous.

She pushed open the door of the pharmacy. "Oh, hi," Arielle said. "Hey, the *Vogue* mags came in. They're in a box in the back. I'll get one in a minute."

"Cool," Emily said. "I'll take one. But I wanted to ask Mr. Kepler about the frames."

"Oh, that's right. I meant to mention it to him. Do you want me to?"

"Yes." Emily nearly gasped. Anything so she didn't have to ask him.

"I'll be right back." Arielle headed toward the pharmacy counter, and Emily turned into the magazine aisle and picked up last month's *Seventeen* magazine. It was all summer outfits—miniskirts and shorts. She thumbed all the way through to the end. What was taking Arielle so long?

The bell rang, and there was a clatter at the front door. Emily stuck her head around the corner of the shelf and then retreated in a hurry. Another customer had just entered and called out, "Hello? Can I get some service?"

"I'll be right there," Arielle called out from the back of the store. A moment later she stopped beside Emily. "Go talk to Mr. Kepler—he thinks it's a good idea. He just has a few questions."

Emily's heart raced as she walked toward the back. Mr. Kepler stood behind the counter, looking through his reading glasses. "Nice to see you again, Emily. Sounds like you could use my help." He smiled, taking off his glasses.

"I'm all for you taking those frames off my hands. What I'll need is a receipt so I can deduct them from my taxes. And some sort of acknowledgment."

"Acknowledgment?" Emily wasn't sure what he meant.

"Yes. It could be verbal, a public statement made at the nursing home. Or written out on a placard to hang on the wall."

"Okay." She could do that.

Mr. Kepler extended his hand. "Then it's a deal. And the sooner you can take the frames—there are five boxes of them—the better. I need the room."

"I'll call my grandmother," Emily said, and then she thanked Mr. Kepler sincerely. Fortunately she had her cell; maybe Grandma could pick up her and the frames and she could coordinate the painting party tomorrow.

Arielle was ringing up her customer as Emily slipped out the door. She dialed the nursing home number but it went straight to voice mail. She tried a second and then a third time, finally leaving a message.

She shoved her phone into her backpack and headed into the store to tell Arielle she'd be back for the frames. It looked like she was walking to the nursing home after all.

Chapter Nineteen

"Two hundred forty!" Red called out. "That's my best score ever."

He laughed as he handed the control to Charlotte. "If my old bowling team back in Boston could only see me now." He stretched his back and then picked up his cane.

"Congratulations," Charlotte said. She was surprised that the game actually required some skill. People who had bowled before and had good form did better than those who hadn't—and, for the most part, did better than they had ever done before.

"How about a round of golf before dinner?" Ruth asked Red.

Red leaned on his cane. "You're determined to keep me humble, aren't you, Ruth?"

Charlotte handed the controller back to Red, and Ruth picked up the other one from the coffee table. Ruth certainly had the game of golf down; it was obvious she had been very good in her day.

Charlotte glanced at her watch as the other residents shuffled out of the room and Red and Ruth started their game. Four thirty. She could be home by five, before Bob started getting too anxious about dinner. She had pork chops thawing, and it would only take a short time to broil them. As she headed toward the stairs, she heard Emily's voice in the lobby, and then there she was, running up the stairs, her face flushed.

"Emily, is everything okay?"

She nodded and stopped in the middle of the staircase. "But I need your help. Mr. Kepler said he'd donate the frames—we just need to pick them up now. And then we can paint them tomorrow."

"Slow down, Emily." It had turned out to be quite the project.

"Oh, and we need to go by Aunt Rosemary's—she's going to donate paint." Emily exhaled. "I should have stopped by there on the way here. I tried to call, to see if you'd come to the pharmacy, but the phone went straight to voice mail each time."

Charlotte stole a look at Diane chatting on the phone at the receptionist's desk. "Did you leave a message?"

Emily nodded. "Yep."

Charlotte started down the stairs. Diane needed to be more attentive to her job; that was for sure. But was it Charlotte's place to say anything? "Let's get going. I want to get home as soon as possible."

Actually, painting the frames tomorrow was a great idea. Emily followed her into the activity director's office and Charlotte collected her purse. "We'll have to have the residents choose photos to go into the frames. And we may have to enlarge some of them, like Arielle said. Have you thought about how to pay for that?"

"Pay?" Emily asked.

Charlotte nodded. "For enlargements."

"Can't the residents pay for that? I'm already scraping together the frames and paints." Emily tightened her grip on her book bag.

"We'll see," Charlotte said. She wasn't sure if some of the residents had extra cash for things like that or not. "We also may need to contact relatives of the residents who don't have photos here and put their photos up at a later date."

Emily sank down into the chair by the desk. "This is getting so complicated."

Charlotte had to coax Emily up and out the door. She didn't want to take the time to talk to Diane, but she needed to. She tried to be diplomatic, to say how important it was not to tie up the phone.

Diane's eyes narrowed. "I was making business phone calls."

"Nursing home business?"

"Yes," Diane said.

"About?" Charlotte asked.

"The newsletter."

Charlotte tried to smile. Was Diane still miffed that Oscar Smith had assigned her that duty?

Diane's sour face turned into a smile as a man dressed in a suit came through the door and approached the desk. Charlotte didn't recognize him. "I'm here to see Ruth Blake," he said.

Diane smiled. "I remember you."

The man nodded. "I'm early—she's not expecting me until this evening."

"Please sign in," Diane said, pointing toward the clipboard on the counter.

"She's in the activities room," Charlotte said, curious as to who the man was. "I can take you up."

"That's okay. I can find my way."

"Left at the top of the staircase," Charlotte said. The man took the stairs two at a time.

Diane stood and leaned forward, peering up the stairs, and then sat back down. "That's Ruth's lawyer, from Grand Island. He only comes when Ruth thinks she's about to keel over."

"Diane—"

"It's true. In fact, you'd better run up the stairs and check on Red. He's probably about ready to have a heart attack."

Charlotte shook her head.

"No, really," Diane said. "Last time the lawyer came, Red was in a funk for days."

Charlotte shook her head. She was not going to get involved in this conversation. "We're going to paint frames tomorrow. Emily is organizing the activity."

"Oh." Diane drummed her fingernails on the desktop. "Well, I'll be finishing up the newsletter."

Charlotte tried to smile, but her face felt frozen. She almost wished she'd said she would do the newsletter; it would have been easier than taking Diane's grief. She glanced at the clock above the desk. 4:40. She walked to the middle of the lobby and looked up to the mezzanine, but she couldn't see Red. Maybe the lawyer was talking with Ruth in the activities room, in front of Red.

She hurried back to the lobby. "Come on, Emily," she said. "Let's get going."

In just a few minutes they were at the pharmacy,

loading the boxes with Arielle's help. Mr. Kepler came out from behind the counter, and Charlotte thanked him.

"Actually, considering all the business I get from Bedford Gardens, I should do more for the place." He chuckled. "I'd just never thought about it until Emily asked me."

More? Charlotte, in an instant, decided to broach the subject of the photos. "Enlarging photos of the residents is part of this project. Could you help with that?"

Emily and Arielle approached just as Charlotte asked.

Mr. Kepler raised his eyebrows. "Well, maybe we could work out a discount."

"I could volunteer my time to make the enlargements," Arielle said.

"And I could help," Emily said.

Mr. Kepler crossed his arms and then smiled. "That's a great idea," he said. "I'd be happy to donate the materials."

Charlotte thanked him again and hustled Emily out the door, calling out a good-bye to Arielle. She glanced at her watch again. Five o'clock. She'd be lucky to have dinner on the table by six.

CHARLOTTE HURRIED INTO THE HOUSE, checking to make sure the pork chops had thawed, and then on into the family room. Bob sat in his chair with eyes closed, his reading glasses sliding down his nose, and the *Bedford Leader* in his hands. Christopher stared blankly at the computer screen.

"Hi," Charlotte said.

"Oh." Christopher looked up, surprised to see her. Then his eyes reverted back to the screen.

"What are you working on?"

"Interview questions." He yawned. "But I keep getting stuck. It's like I can't decide what to write about. Should I write about Ruth's life? Or Red's life? Or about you helping out there? Or about what they do there now?"

Charlotte took a deep breath. She didn't have time to listen to Christopher at the moment; she wanted to get started on dinner, but she knew she *needed* to listen. "What did Rick Barnes say to you? As far as choosing a topic?"

"To write about what interests me."

"What interests you most about the nursing home?"

His eyes lit up. "The Wii."

That figured. "Well, can you write about that?"

His face fell. "Everyone already knows about Wiis. Either they have one or they want one."

"But they might not know why a group of elderly people would like to play the Wii." Charlotte straightened the pillows on the couch.

"What do you mean?"

"Well, did you know that Red played baseball in the minors?"

"What's the minors?"

"There's Major League Baseball, and then the minor league is the next level down. You know, the San Diego Padres are a Major League Baseball team. The minors are where the majors get some of their players."

"Cool."

"And Ruth used to play golf with her husband all over the country."

"Really?"

Charlotte nodded.

"But this is due on Wednesday." He slumped against the computer chair.

"Come tomorrow after school with Emily. Ask Ruth and Red what it's like to play the Wii now."

Christopher pushed his palms against either side of his head. "Maybe I'll do that," he said. "But then that would only give me tomorrow evening to write the article." Christopher flung his head from side to side. "I'm going crazy."

"Can I go with you?" Emily collapsed on the couch, a tube of paint in one hand and a metal frame in the other. "School just started and already I feel stressed out."

Bob shifted in his chair and let out a snore.

"*Shh,*" Christopher said, spinning back around to the computer. "Don't wake him. He's been really grumpy."

How grumpy had Bob been? "Come set the table, Emily." Charlotte turned on her heels.

"Why do I always have to set the table?" Emily grabbed a pillow and hugged it tight. "I'm tired."

"We're all tired," Charlotte said.

"Where's Sam? He's not tired. He's not doing anything."

"He went for a drive," Christopher said.

"What?" Charlotte spun around.

"A drive," Christopher repeated.

"Who gave him permission?"

"Grandpa," Christopher kept his eyes on the computer screen. "Kind of."

AS THEY SAT DOWN TO DINNER, Charlotte asked Bob when he expected Sam back.

"Sam?" Bob scratched his head behind his ear.

"Sam. Christopher said you gave him permission to go for a drive."

Bob unfolded his napkin and then glanced at Christopher.

"Nightfall," Christopher whispered loudly.

"Nightfall?" Charlotte blurted out. "Where did he go?"

Bob shrugged and then looked at Christopher again.

"Sam was mumbling—I couldn't hear. I just heard Grandpa say, 'Sure. Just be home by nightfall.'"

Bob blushed and then clammed up, and the four of them ate in silence. Should Charlotte start calling Sam's friends? Jake and Paul? What about Arielle? Would he go to her house? Probably not. After all, she and Emily had been with Arielle at the pharmacy at about the time Sam would have left to go into town. She imagined him full of teenage angst, speeding along a country road.

"I'll call him on his cell after dinner," Charlotte said.

"Can't." Christopher swallowed before he spoke again. "He left it on the computer desk."

Charlotte took a deep breath. Pete was still out working in the fields, but she would ask him if he had any idea where Sam went when he came in.

Christopher asked to be excused first to go work on his interview questions.

Charlotte shook her head. "We haven't done our Bible reading yet, and besides, I need you and Emily to put the food away and do the dishes."

"Grandma," Emily wailed, "I have a ton of homework to do."

"Then do the dishes quickly."

Bob pushed his chair back.

"Where are you going?" Charlotte asked.

Bob stood and put his hands against the table. "To my chair, where I can dream about my old life." Then he stalked away from the table.

Christopher looked confused, and Emily looked mortified. "What does he mean?" she asked.

"He's just tired, that's all." Charlotte began stacking the plates. What *did* he mean?

"But he didn't read out of the Bible storybook." Christopher licked his fork.

"Did he mean before we came?" Emily asked.

Charlotte shook her head. "No. It was directed toward me, before I was working." But she wasn't so sure. When she went into the family room to talk things through with Bob, he was asleep in his chair again, or at least he appeared to be, his reading glasses back on his nose.

CHARLOTTE RETREATED to the garden after Emily and Christopher got started on the dishes. The crookneck squash needed watering, and the pole beans had grown half a foot in the last few days. She turned the water on at the spigot by the back door and pulled the hose over to the squash. And the weeds! How had that happened? She'd been trying to weed some each morning after the kids left for school but obviously it wasn't enough.

The dahlias needed to be deadheaded and the roses were drooping too. Bob, the children, the flowers, the vegetables—

all of them felt neglected. Toby approached her with a whimper. "Oh, come here, girl," Charlotte said, kneeling down on the lawn. "You haven't had any attention either, have you?" Charlotte rubbed the dog's neck and then ran her hand along the dog's backbone.

Toby rolled over onto her back, and Charlotte sat down on the grass and rubbed the dog's stomach, fingering the mats in her long hair. She or Christopher needed to brush the dog. Poor thing.

Charlotte stood and turned off the water and then began weeding between the tomato plants. She should have read out of the Bible storybook to the kids. That would have set a better example than letting it go. It didn't have to be Bob who always did the reading. She tossed the weeds into a pile on the lawn.

And she shouldn't have gotten so annoyed with him for not remembering where Sam said he was going. What was Sam thinking, asking his sleeping grandfather for permission? Actually, that was probably exactly what Sam was thinking.

It was almost as bad as sneaking out, which was something both Denise and Pete used to do. And Sam had done that too last winter. She took a deep breath. She didn't want to go through that again. He had to understand that if they were going to trust him, he had to be honest with them.

Her frustration grew as she moved over a row to the pole beans. The weeds stuck up among the plants. She reached down and grabbed a bunch and pulled. Up came the weeds with a huge clump of dirt attached. She shook it, sending a cloud of dust into the air. Sam had said he would talk with

Mr. Santos, but he hadn't, at least not as far she knew. Why couldn't he just apply himself?

Pete's pickup turned into the driveway, and he waved as he parked it. "Howdy," he called out, jumping down from his pickup. Dried mud streaked his face and clothes. He spread his hands out. "I had a wrestling match with an irrigation pipe and lost. Hey, I'm starved. When's dinner?"

Charlotte straightened up, stretching her back as she did. "About an hour ago." And it was late at that.

"Really." Pete held his watch up in front of his face. "My watch musta quit working."

"There are leftover pork chops. Emily and Christopher are cleaning up." Boy, it seemed like she'd been cooking a lot of chops lately; they were easy.

"I passed Sam coming back from the field, headed south. He was cooking along—didn't even seem to see me."

"Really?"

"What's he up to?"

Charlotte almost said, "Ask Dad," but caught herself before the words tumbled out. "I'm not sure. I was hoping you would know." He'd been out of sorts since he and Arielle fell out. She'd hoped that going to Ruth's on Saturday morning would straighten everything out, but it seemed it hadn't. Arielle was hard to read, and Sam was impossible.

"Well, I'm going to go get a chop and then get cleaned up."

"Can you do the milking?" Charlotte asked.

A look of annoyance crossed Pete's face as he said he'd do it, but could she take over, for sure, once soybean harvest started? "Because," he said, "I can't do everything around here."

Charlotte turned back to the garden, taking her shears out of her back pocket and starting on the dahlias. Everyone was in a bad mood. No wonder she hadn't worked off the farm all these years. But to be honest, she was really enjoying her time at Bedford Gardens. If it turned into a permanent position, could she make it work?

CHARLOTTE WAS STANDING at the kitchen sink straining the milk, when Sam's car turned into the driveway at dusk. She pulled the curtain back and watched as he parked. He waited a minute before he opened the door, as if he were waiting for a song on the radio to finish. When he unfolded his body from the car, straightening up all at once, she was surprised at how tall he looked. It seemed like he grew each day.

Christopher and Toby jogged toward him, and Christopher said something but Sam didn't respond. He headed toward the back door and opened it as Charlotte poured the milk into the pitcher.

"Where've you been, Sam?" she asked.

"Around." He kicked off his shoes.

"Where did you tell Grandpa you were going?"

"For a drive."

"There are leftover pork chops." Maybe. Unless Pete ate all of them. "Gas is too expensive to just drive around for no reason."

He popped the lid off the container. "I can't think here. It's too claustrophobic."

If he was feeling so claustrophobic, why wasn't he willing to look at colleges? She nearly broke her promise to herself not to ask if he'd talked with Mr. Santos. He had one week until soccer tryouts.

Sam put a pork chop on a plate.

"How about some salad and a roll?"

"No thanks." He grabbed a fork and knife and headed over to the table.

"Christopher and Emily need to go to the nursing home after school tomorrow, and I could use your help too."

"Will Arielle be there?"

Charlotte nodded. Tuesday was the day Arielle stayed late.

"Then I won't be there." Sam began cutting his meat with a vengeance.

"I'll still need you to give Emily and Christopher a ride."

Sam shoved the meat into his mouth. "You working is getting to be a real pain."

Chapter Twenty

Emily grabbed the bag of paints from the floor of Sam's 240-Z and flung the door open as Sam pulled up in front of the nursing home.

"How come you're not coming in?" Christopher asked Sam.

"'Cuz." Sam flipped his head away from them.

"'Cuz he and Arielle had a fight." Emily stepped from the car.

"Why?"

"That's the million-dollar question. Why would Sam be mean to Arielle? No one can figure it out."

Sam revved the engine and called out, "I'm really getting tired of your smart mouth."

Christopher scrambled out of the car.

"Knock it off," Emily said to Sam. "Stop being such a jerk."

Sam saluted her and started easing the car backward as Christopher slammed the door.

"What's with him?" Christopher asked as they headed toward the front door.

"Girl problems. Plus Mr. Santos is still out sick so he can't talk with him about colleges. He keeps digging one hole after another."

They pushed through the door and were greeted by Grandma. "Here they are!"

The residents sat around the craft tables, each with a frame in front of them. Emily opened the paper bag of paint and began distributing the squeeze bottles around the tables.

"Hey, I have most of the photos," Arielle said. "Connie and the other aides got them from the residents' rooms. They only had to call a couple of the families to help us out." She held up a stack of pictures. "You can help me process them tomorrow."

"Cool," Emily said. "May I look?"

Arielle handed her the photos and Emily began thumbing through them. She stopped at a photo of a young woman with jet black hair, wearing a red dress with a flared skirt standing in front of a cream-colored car. "I think this is Aggie," she said, holding it up.

Arielle nodded. "Wasn't she beautiful?"

"And look at that dress." Emily held the photo closer. It looked like the hem of the skirt was embroidered. She flipped the picture over and on the back she read, "Agnes, 1951, off to college."

"Aggie," Emily said, walking around the table to the woman. "You were gorgeous."

Aggie nodded. "So they say," she whispered.

"Where did you go to college?"

"South Dakota. On a chemistry scholarship."

"You're kidding?" Emily looked at the photo again. *1951.* That was so long ago.

Next was a photo of a man in a baseball uniform. "Red, is this you?" She turned the photo around.

Red smiled. "That's me. Yours truly."

Bright red hair, obvious even though the picture's colors had faded, stuck out from under the baseball cap. He was wound up, ready to pitch.

"And who is this?" Emily asked, holding up a photo of a woman with long dark hair wearing a poodle skirt. "No, don't tell me. It's you, Betty. Right?"

Betty beamed and Emily started leafing through the rest of the photos, looking for Ruth's, but she couldn't find anyone that looked classy enough to be Ruth.

"Where's your photo?" she asked, bending over.

"Oh, that," Ruth said. "I'm still looking."

Aggie squeezed the bottle of paint and a big glob squirted out.

"Oops," Emily said. "Let me help." She handed Arielle the stack of photos and hurried around to help the disabled woman.

"Christopher," Ruth said, pushing the frame in front of her and folding her hands on the table. "Your grandmother said you wanted to interview me."

Christopher nodded. "I wanted to ask you about golfing—from before, you know."

Ruth laughed. "From when I was on the outside?"

Christopher nodded. "And why you like the Wii now. And Mr. Red too, but about baseball."

"Well," Red said, "you know how I like to talk about baseball—that all-American sport."

Ruth smiled demurely. "Come on, Christopher. Let's go sit in the easy chairs. Away from any distractions."

Emily cleaned up the glob of paint on the table in front

of Aggie and then squeezed the tube of royal blue paint until it flowed evenly. "There," she said, handing the paint to the woman.

The residents worked for half an hour, first deciding what motifs they wanted on their frames and then carefully squirting the paint on.

"It's hard to define your life with a symbol," Red said, carefully outlining the form of a baseball.

"Well, don't think of it as a definition," Emily said. "Think of it as a glimpse."

Red nodded.

Aggie worked carefully, squirting out an oval shape and then another overlapping it. She continued on.

Emily tilted her head, trying to figure out what the woman was doing. "Oh, it's an atom," she said.

Aggie smiled.

"Aggie, did you graduate from college?"

"Sure did," she whispered. "And I taught high school chemistry for thirty years afterward. Just took off enough time to get my daughter into school."

Emily shook her head. She didn't know that many women who taught chemistry, not even now. She glanced around the lobby. Ruth and Christopher chuckled together in the far corner. The residents who were doing the art project were all enjoying themselves—it seemed to be the perfect project. Arielle was thumbing through the photos one more time. Grandma was moving the painted frames to a table against the window to dry. Emily took out her cell phone and began snapping pictures. She needed to document the project for Ms. Carey.

"Your turn," Ruth said to Red, approaching the table.

Red limped over to the easy chairs where Christopher waited, and Ruth sat back down at the table. "Your brother needs a photo for the newspaper—one of me playing golf." She sighed. "And to think I almost got out of having to cough up a photo."

"But what about one for your frame? Weren't you going to do that?" Emily asked.

"Actually . . . ," Ruth said.

Emily crossed her arms. "What?" Ruth was the last person she expected to not cooperate. The old woman shrugged and gave Emily a sheepish smile as she headed across the lobby to the stairs.

CHRISTOPHER SAT AT THE COMPUTER with his article in front of him: "Seniors Relive Sports Through Wii." Grandma had helped him with the headline. He couldn't decide whether to start the article with Ruth's story or Red's. Ruth had started golfing to spend more time with her husband, who was a geologist. They had lived all over the West. Red had played college baseball and then for a Red Sox farm team. His dream had been to play pro ball, but he never made it. He didn't seem that disappointed though.

Grandma sat in her chair, staring straight ahead. She seemed tired.

"Grandma," Christopher said, spinning around in the computer chair, "is Red the best Wii baseball player at Bedford Gardens?"

Grandma nodded. "And Ruth is the best golfer. That's the thing about Wii; real-life skills transfer over to the game."

"Why doesn't Ruth just play real golf? There's a course in Harding."

"She's too ill," Grandma said. "It would be too hard for her to walk around the course."

"She doesn't seem ill."

"She has congestive heart failure."

"What's that?"

"Her heart isn't working as well as yours or mine, which makes her tire easily," Grandma said.

"Oh. Is she going to die?" Christopher spun back around to the computer.

"Sometime—but probably not soon."

Christopher wondered if Grandma was telling the truth. Lots of times grown-ups said stuff like that just to make you feel better. He began writing about Ruth moving to the United States after World War II and how she golfed for the first time on a little course in northern California, surprising her husband with how far she could hit the ball. It sounded like a fun game, walking around on nice green grass or, better yet, driving around in a cart and hitting a ball. It didn't sound that hard. It actually sounded a lot easier than baseball. Christopher had tried that in PE without much luck.

Maybe he could play Wii golf with Ruth sometime and see if he liked it. Maybe Sam would take him to Bedford Gardens next Monday.

"When is Sam getting home?" Christopher asked.

Grandma shrugged and picked up her embroidery.

It was a little weird how Sam had been going off by himself. It wasn't like him. As much as Christopher liked going to the nursing home, he wished things were back to normal, that Grandma was home when he got back from school and that Sam and Emily were with him. He was ready for things to be normal again, or at least close to normal.

Grandpa let out a snore from his chair. Grandma and Grandpa weren't talking much, and that worried him too. What if they got divorced the way his mom and dad had? Then what?

SAM SLOWED AS HE APPROACHED Arielle's house and then sped up again when he saw her dad's pickup in the driveway. He'd told Grandma he was going to Jake's house, and he'd intended to, but then he didn't. Instead he'd kicked his soccer ball against the cement playground wall at the grade school. And now here he was, stalking Arielle. He shivered.

"Get a grip, Sam," he muttered. "Get a grip."

Maybe he was, as Emily said, just a jerk. Maybe he was like his dad. Maybe he didn't have it in him to be a decent man.

He turned onto Oldham Street and slowed by the fire station. Uncle Pete's truck was in front; it was Tuesday evening, the weekly meeting night. The doors were open and the engine was parked on the cement pad, sparkling in the evening light. He envied the men inside. All of them belonged; all of them had a purpose. He still wanted to join when he was old enough. At least for now, when he was with Arielle he felt like he belonged, sort of, at least more than he had before. He turned on Farnam Street and headed south.

But now he felt lost again, and it didn't help that everyone at school was talking behind his back. He pulled alongside Morley Park and turned off his engine, watching the bats fly out of the trees and into the darkening sky. *Dusk*. That was what Grandma called it. He thought it was the most depressing time of the day. He walked toward the gazebo in the middle of the park and climbed the stairs.

"Sam, is that you?" It was Arielle, walking toward him.

"Oh, hi," he said, with no emotion. "What's up?"

Arielle stopped at the gazebo, and Sam looked down at her. "I needed to get out of the house."

"Oh."

"So how are you doing?"

"Fine." Sam stuffed his hands into the pockets of his jeans, trying to think of something to say.

"That was fun on Saturday morning, watching the game," she said as she met Sam up on the gazebo.

Sam nodded.

"I sure hope you can play on the Harding team."

Sam shrugged.

Arielle stomped her foot on the concrete floor of the gazebo.

He stepped backward. What was she doing?

"Sam Slater, this is what drives me nuts about you."

Was she really that angry? He tried to speak, but nothing came out.

"You act like you don't care about anything," she said. "But it's weird. At the same time you care too much about what other people think." Her dangly earrings swung back and forth as she spoke.

Sam tilted his head, confused. It felt like she was firing a gun at him.

"You care about what Jake thinks, and that makes you dishonest. That's one thing." She took a breath. "Then you want something, like soccer, but you won't do what you need to do to make it happen."

"I can't help it that Mr. Santos has scarlet fever."

"Have you talked to anyone in the office? Have you asked if you can call him at home? Have you even gone online and made a list of colleges?"

Sam shrugged.

She sighed. He liked it better when she stomped her foot. "I have to get going." She turned without saying good-bye, taking the stairs of the gazebo two at a time.

Sam leaned over the railing. "Do you want a ride?"

"No!" Arielle shot back over her shoulder and then started to run.

Sam waited in the gazebo until she reached the street. Why was she so mad at him? She had been so nice before. He walked toward his car, tipping his head to see a swarm of bats flying out of the treetops and then back in.

When he reached the house, Grandma and Grandpa were both in the family room—wide awake, for a change. The windows and door were all open and the electric fan was on, whirring back and forth.

Sam sat down at the computer and stared at the screen.

What colleges was he interested in? He'd been interested in Harding State when Arielle was, but if she was going to go to a college in Tennessee, then he wasn't sure if he wanted to go to school in Harding. San Diego would be cool, but he wouldn't have in-state tuition anymore, so that would be tough to pay for. It was hard to think that far ahead. Was he going to have to take out loans to pay for college? What if he didn't get a job after he graduated? Or worse, what if he didn't graduate? He covered his face with his hands.

"Son, did you talk to the counselor today?" Grandpa asked.

"No." Sam pulled his hands down, stretching his skin with his fingers. He didn't turn around as he spoke.

"And why not?"

Grandma stirred in her chair.

Sam spun around. "He's out sick with scarlet fever."

"Oh, dear," Grandma said.

"He's been out for days," Sam said. "Almost a week." That wasn't quite true. It had been three days so far.

"Well." Grandpa stood, slipping his reading glasses into the pocket of his shirt. "You had time before that to talk to him. Our deal still stands."

Sam spun back around to the computer. It was easy for Arielle to go into the office and ask questions. She knew all the women in the office, and they liked her. It wasn't so easy for him.

None of this was fair. He spun back around and faced Grandpa. "What am I supposed to do?" His voice rose as he spoke. "The guy is really sick. It's not my fault."

Grandpa sat up straight. "Don't raise your voice with me, young man."

Young man? Sam vaulted from the chair and crashed through the living room to the front door of the house. He banged it open and stomped out onto the porch. He wanted to hit something. He punched his fist into the palm of his other hand and fled down the front stairs. None of this was fair.

SAM STOPPED AT MR. SANTOS'S office door the next morning and pressed his nose against the frosted glass. The office was dark inside, again. He'd been hoping the guy would show up, by magic or something.

He exhaled slowly and then turned on his heels. Arielle had said the office ladies were really nice, that they had helped her. They hadn't been nice to him before, but maybe if he asked about college they would be.

He shuffled down the hall with his head down, avoiding looking at Arielle as he passed by her locker, although he was aware of her talking with Halley. They paused as he went by, and he could feel their eyes on him.

He pushed through the office door. The older office lady was on the phone, and three freshmen were waiting to speak to her. Sam crossed his arms. Why was Grandpa insisting on this? It seemed as if they should be happy for him to play soccer.

It all felt like too much pressure. The lady hung up the phone and asked the first freshman what she needed. The girl began to whisper something.

"I need you to speak up," the woman belted out.

The girl's voice increased a little. "I forgot my locker combination."

Sam frowned. To his disgust, the other two freshmen had forgotten their locker combinations too.

By the time it was his turn, the woman looked grumpier than ever. "What do you need?" she barked.

"I have some questions about colleges," Sam stammered.

"Oh, really?" She leaned against the counter. "Have you talked to Mr. Santos?"

"He's out sick."

"I know. I meant before, when school first started."

Sam shook his head.

"Well, that's a shame." She picked up a file and opened it.

"Why?" Sam wanted to flee out the door.

She looked at him again. "Well, your grades, for one thing. They're not that great, right? That limits your options."

Sam's face flushed. He'd been doing better.

"I'm not sure what to tell you," she said. "Mr. Santos might be able to help you figure it out, but I can't." She glanced back down at the file.

He backed out of the door without saying thank you and turned abruptly, nearly knocking Arielle over.

"Oh. Excuse me," he said, stepping away quickly.

"You okay?" she asked.

He didn't stop to answer. Why had he bothered? Were his grades really that bad? Was college out of the question? If so, then soccer probably was too.

Chapter Twenty-One

The phone began to ring just as Charlotte opened the back door. She really should let it go and get on her way to the nursing home. After all, it was Wednesday, tea day, but then she might need to find time in the evening to return the call.

It was Hannah. "Charlotte, are you still alive?"

"Barely."

"I'm dying for a walk and a good talk. How about this evening?"

Charlotte glanced at the calendar. There was nothing on it. "I think I can do that." Would Bob mind? He'd been so grumpy, but yesterday she'd spent the whole evening with him in the family room, and he'd hardly said a word.

"How about seven thirty?"

"Sounds good." Charlotte said good-bye and headed to the car. Spending time with Hannah would be good for her; she just hoped Bob and the kids weren't too needy tonight.

"Are you off, then?" Bob asked, wiping a wrench on a rag as he leaned against the truck.

"Yes. I'll be home by six."

He waved and retreated back under the hood. She was tempted to ask him if he wanted to tag along but then suppressed a giggle. It was hard to imagine Bob at a tea.

As she stopped to pull onto the highway, Pete slowed his pickup to a stop. "How's the career woman?" he asked.

She ignored the "career" jab. His baseball cap was on backward, and he looked tired. She hadn't seen him much in the last few days, but honestly, in her busyness, she'd hardly missed him.

"How are the kids doing?" Pete asked.

"A little out of sorts right now," she answered. "Especially Sam. Do you think you can get him to help you this afternoon? It would be good for him to be busier, to not have so much time to mope."

Pete nodded. "I have about a million things that need to be done around here. I'll catch him after school."

Charlotte continued on into town. The cook had ordered cookies for the tea. Charlotte would need to set the tables and make the tea. She hoped Stephanie would be there with the baby. Charlotte wanted an update on Stephanie's husband's job situation.

What would Charlotte do if Oscar asked her to take the position permanently? Some days she thought it would be a great idea and others she wasn't as sure. Well . . . She slowed as she entered the city limits. That was nothing to think about now, but if she didn't keep the job she would miss it. She found working at the nursing home fulfilling in a way far different from working at home.

Christopher planned to come after school to help with the tea, but Emily was going to the pharmacy with Arielle to copy the photos. In fact, Arielle wasn't helping at the nursing home at all today.

Honestly, the teas were too much. They should be a once-a-month event at the most, not weekly. She knew Ruth enjoyed them, along with the other women, but they were too hard on the staff.

Sam had said he'd give Christopher a ride to the nursing home. She hoped he'd remember. She preferred it when the children were all together instead of off in three different directions.

AS THE RESIDENTS SAT DOWN and Charlotte hurried around pouring tea, Ruth came down the stairs carrying a photograph and then approached Charlotte with it.

"Thank you," Charlotte said. "Could you put it on my desk? I'll give it to Emily."

"Oh no, dear, it's for Christopher. For his article."

"Oh." Charlotte craned her neck to see the photo. The black-and-white print was of a thirty-something Ruth standing on a putting green wearing a white skirt and blouse, ready to swing. Her hair hung around her shoulders in soft curls, and she was looking at the photographer, smiling. "Ruth, what a beautiful picture."

"Oh, it will do," Ruth said. "I was never very photogenic."

"Why don't I have Emily use this for your door photo too?"

Ruth shook her head. "Not yet, please." She headed to her seat beside Stephanie and baby Lillian.

"Do you have any news about your hubby's job situation?" Ruth asked.

"He had an interview last Friday," Stephanie answered. It seemed she was eager to change the subject. "He should hear about it any day now."

Charlotte poured tea across the table for Aggie.

"Have you heard from your nephew recently?" Stephanie asked Ruth.

Ruth's face lit up in a smile. "I had an e-mail just this morning. He had a few questions for me—which I promptly answered."

The baby began to fuss. Ruth put out her arms for the little one and then stood with ease and began swaying back and forth. "There's nothing in the world like you, is there, little Lillian?" she cooed. "Nothing at all."

CHARLOTTE WIPED DOWN the counters after the kids had finished up the dishes. Toby began to bark, and Charlotte looked out the window. Sure enough, Hannah was pulling into the driveway.

Charlotte wiped her hands on a dishtowel and hurried to the back door. "I just need to tell Bob I'm going," she called out to Hannah as her friend climbed from her truck.

"Grandma!" Christopher rushed toward her. "I need you to read the rewrite of my article. Miss Luka said to have you edit it—we're doing the layouts tomorrow and then copying it on Friday morning."

"Leave it on the table. I'll read it when I get back." Which meant Christopher would have to make the changes in the morning.

"Where are you going?" Christopher asked.

"On a walk with Hannah." Charlotte glanced toward her friend. Wasn't it obvious?

"Can I go with you?" Christopher threw a stick for Toby.

"Um . . ." *No!* Charlotte wanted to shout. This was her time. "You need to get a bath, Christopher."

He frowned. "I'd rather go for a walk."

Charlotte shrugged her shoulders and turned toward the shed. "Bob," she called out, walking over to him, "I'm leaving."

He poked his head out from under the hood of the truck. "Where are you going?"

"On a walk with Hannah."

Bob shook his head.

"I told you at dinner."

He poked his head back under the hood. Didn't he remember? "Honey," she said, "I'll only be gone an hour."

He glanced at his watch. "In an hour, I'll probably be asleep."

"So stay awake." She pecked a kiss on his cheek. It wouldn't matter if he were awake. She would need to read Christopher's article, and it seemed that Emily always got talky right before bedtime—before Charlotte's bedtime anyway. It was go, go, go until the minute she dropped into bed, and by then Bob was usually already snoring up a storm. Maybe she shouldn't have said yes to a walk tonight.

"How are you doing?" Hannah asked as they headed by the windbreak of poplar trees with Toby trotting beside them.

"Oh, I'm feeling a little overwhelmed."

"What have they decided at Bedford Gardens?"

"Pardon?"

"About Stephanie's position?"

Charlotte shook her head. "I haven't heard anything."

"I was in town just before dinnertime, at Mel's Place. I heard Stephanie's husband got a job in Grand Island. She's resigning as the activity director."

"Oh," was all Charlotte could say. They turned on the path toward the creek, making their way alongside the wheat stubble.

"I'm sorry if I jumped the gun," Hannah said. "But I really didn't think it was a rumor. Oscar Smith was in at Mel's Place. He was complaining about how hard it is to keep a business running these days."

"Oh," Charlotte said again. What were her chances of getting hired permanently? And if she did, what were the chances that she could make it all work? They left the field and walked along the bank of the creek. The air was significantly cooler as they ducked under the branches of the willow trees. Toby ran ahead and then careered down into the creek, splashing in the water and then racing back toward Charlotte and Hannah, shaking herself furiously.

"Oh!" Hannah screamed as she stepped backward.

"Toby," Charlotte scolded, but the dog was running ahead again.

A minute later they were talking about the upcoming soybean harvest and the weather, about how hot it had been. Hannah asked about the grandkids, and Charlotte filled her in, one by one, leaving Sam for last.

"So what's he going to do?" Hannah asked after Charlotte

had explained Bob's requirement that Sam look into colleges before trying out for the soccer team.

"You know it's not that much—all he has to do is start gathering information. I'm beginning to think he doesn't really want to play soccer," Charlotte said. "Maybe he got what he needed today though. He helped Pete after school and then they ran to Harding for a part for the combine so I haven't talked with him today." The women continued along the creek, trailing Toby.

Forty minutes later, Pete's pickup passed the women as they walked back up the driveway to the house. Sam climbed down from the passenger seat with a McDonald's bag in his hands, looking dejected.

"What's with Sam?" Charlotte asked Pete as her grandson shuffled toward the house.

Pete shrugged. "He seemed okay until I drove him by the practice field in Harding, where his tryouts will be. Then he got all quiet."

Obviously Sam hadn't talked to Mr. Santos or anyone else about college today.

Charlotte sighed and hugged Hannah, telling her friend good-bye.

AFTER EDITING CHRISTOPHER'S ARTICLE about Ruth, Red, and the world of Wii sports at Bedford Gardens, Charlotte crawled into bed and then sat up to push the blanket back. It was much too hot for any added weight. The sheet was plenty. She settled her head onto her pillow and then waited for Bob to snore, but there was only silence.

Well, nearly silence. Pete was still working on the combine. She could hear the clink of his tools, and the light from the shed shone in their bedroom window. She had insisted that Sam come into the house right before she went to bed. He was still grumpy, acting as if Mr. Santos having scarlet fever was her fault.

"Char."

She startled.

Bob turned toward her. "Are you awake?"

Of course she was awake.

"How was your walk?" he asked.

"Fine." She couldn't remember the last time he'd asked about one of her activities.

"And how was work today?"

"Okay." She paused. "Actually it was kind of hard. We had another tea, and they're a lot of work." She wanted to tell him about Hannah saying that Stephanie had resigned but she was afraid he might get grouchy.

"It's a lot," Bob said. "I know you're not working very much, but it's made things harder around here. I'll be glad when you're done."

Charlotte bristled. Why was it that doing something she enjoyed upset the balance of the whole family? If Bob decided to do something for ten hours a week, or even a little more, no one would even notice.

"I mean," he said, "if you were volunteering a few hours a week that would be one thing, but going in every day, it's hard on the kids."

Charlotte didn't answer.

"And on me." He turned toward her. "I know you enjoy

it, but I don't think I could handle it if you did this all the time. I liked our life before, before the kids, before you started working. Sure, the kids can't be helped, and don't get me wrong, I am so thankful they're here. But the job?"

Charlotte kicked the sheet off. Was she hot? Or mad?

Bob continued. "The job can be helped. I'm counting the days until you're done." He exhaled. "Except it's kind of hard to count, when you haven't told me when your last day is."

Charlotte sat up in bed. "Robert Stevenson." She kicked her feet over the side of the bed and turned on the bedside lamp.

"What?" Bob sat up too.

"I have supported you your entire life while you did what you love to do—farm. And now, when I finally get a chance to do something I love, you act like this." She stood.

"Char."

She grabbed her robe and headed out to the hall. A minute later she sat on the sofa in the living room, peering out the picture window at the moonlit yard.

"Char?" Bob stood in the doorway.

She turned toward him, a little embarrassed, feeling as if she'd overreacted.

"Has it been that bad?" he asked. "All these years on the farm?"

"No," she said. "It's been fine. It's just that I never had a chance to do what I wanted to do."

"But what about the kids? And the garden? And helping me?"

And the thousands and thousands of meals? And loads of laundry? And trips into town for parts? "I'm out of sorts tonight, but it would be nice to feel I had your support just this once, since I've found something I really enjoy."

He yawned. "Can we talk about this tomorrow?"

She crossed her arms. "I'll be in in a minute." She knew no good would come from a heated, late-night argument with Bob. She also knew life didn't always turn out the way one expected. Still, she felt a little jealous of Arielle and Emily deciding what they wanted to do with their lives. Things were different now. They had more options. More opportunities. Maybe that was what was so frustrating about Sam. She was afraid he wasn't going to take advantage of the opportunities he had.

A minute later Charlotte tossed her bathrobe on the chair and crawled back under the sheet, turning her head toward the window and the lace curtains, backlit by moonlight.

She was too old to be feeling this way. Why couldn't she shake her feelings of regret?

Chapter Twenty-Two

"Look at this." Red stood in the middle of the lobby, waving a piece of paper and leaning against his cane. "Look what Arielle accomplished."

Charlotte stepped out of her office. "What's up, Red?"

"What's going on?" Arielle's voice came from above, where she'd been working on the puzzle. "What did I do, Red?"

He turned and looked up. "All those forms you filled out paid off. My insurance company is going to cover my meds."

"That's great." Arielle's head disappeared, and in a minute she was coming down the staircase and then standing in front of Red, giving him a high five, the paper getting caught between their hands.

"I think you have a gift," Red said. "I think you've found your calling."

Arielle blushed. "Maybe I'll look into social work in college," she said as Emily and Christopher pushed through the door.

"Hhhhmph." It was Emily, clearing her throat, standing over by the table where the picture frames were. "Are we going to do this today? I kind of need to wrap this up so I can get on to other things."

Arielle, Emily, and Charlotte matched up the photos with the frames and began inserting them. Emily counted the pictures. "We're short one."

"Ruth's," Charlotte answered.

"Oh, no," Emily said. "Why didn't we make a copy of the golf photo?"

"She didn't want us to," Charlotte said.

"Why not?" Arielle picked up Aggie's and Red's frames.

"She wouldn't say."

"That's just like her," Red said from the overstuffed chair he sat in across the lobby. Obviously his hearing was fine. "You know those English. They say they're reserved, but really they're stubborn to the end."

"Where is Ruth now?" Emily asked.

"She's been in her room all day. She won't come out." Red turned toward them.

"Maybe I should go check on her," Charlotte said.

"Oh, don't bother. She won't let you in. She's up to something."

CHRISTOPHER FOLLOWED CHARLOTTE up the stairs, waving a piece of paper at her. "Look." He had his school newspaper in his hand. "My article." He handed it to Charlotte at the top of the stairs. It was the lead article, with the photos of Red and Ruth front and center.

"And guess what," Christopher said. "The kids in my class want to come over here for a Wii tournament, and Miss Luka says it's okay with her if it's okay with you."

Charlotte tousled his hair. "That's a great idea, but we'll have to see."

Christopher frowned. "Grandma, this is exactly what Rick Barnes was talking about. About educating people and enlightening them. I've educated my classmates, and now they want to experience what goes on here."

"Well, I'll need to talk with Oscar Smith." She felt a little awkward talking with him, considering what Hannah had told her about Stephanie resigning. She'd been expecting a call all day, hoping he would offer her the job. She actually thought she might take it if he did. Bob would just have to adjust.

"Miss Luka said she could be flexible around the schedule here." Christopher did a little skip as they walked down the hall. "But she said that Tuesday would be the best day."

Tuesday? It was already Friday. That meant she would need to call Oscar today.

She knocked on Ruth's door. After a long minute it opened slightly and then Ruth slipped through, greeting both Charlotte and Christopher.

"I'm not up to visitors today," she said.

Christopher handed her the newspaper.

"Oh, how wonderful," she said, patting his shoulder. "Thank you."

"Ruth," a voice called out.

"Is Connie in there?" Charlotte stepped toward the door. It was the aide's day off.

"Why yes." Ruth smiled. "I've hired her to help me with some things."

"Oh." Charlotte stepped back. "Well, I'll see you on Monday then."

"Splendid," Ruth replied. "Well, then, cheerio."

A minute later Charlotte left Christopher in the lobby

and ducked into Stephanie's office. She might as well call Oscar now. She dialed his cell phone. On the sixth ring he picked up with a gruff hello.

Charlotte asked if he was busy, and he said he was driving between Harding and Grand Island.

Charlotte started, "I was wondering—"

Oscar cut her off. "I've been meaning to call you, to talk about your schedule."

"That's exactly why I was calling."

"Stephanie has resigned, and we need to tighten the budget. So," he said, "Diane will be taking on your duties, and Monday will be your last day."

"Oh," Charlotte said.

"Thank you," Oscar said.

Was he ready to hang up? "Wait," Charlotte said. "I have a couple of questions." She told him about Christopher's class.

"That's fine," Oscar said. "As long as they wash their hands and don't spread any germs around. But I can't pay you for that day."

"I understand," Charlotte said. "Actually, I would like to volunteer a couple of hours one day a week at the nursing home, if that's all right."

There was a beep on the phone. Oscar had another call coming in. "No problem," Oscar said. "Just let me know later what you want to do. I'll have your check ready for you on Monday. Good-bye."

Charlotte hung up the phone. It would be both her first and last check. Well, Bob would be happy that her short working career would be coming to a screeching halt. She retrieved her purse from the drawer and stood.

Arielle was talking to Christopher in the lobby as Charlotte approached. "Mr. Santos will be back on Monday," Arielle said.

"Tryouts are on Tuesday," Christopher said. "Do you think that will give him enough time?"

Arielle sighed. "I hope so."

Charlotte bit her tongue. Maybe this would teach Sam a lesson about procrastinating. She headed over to the receptionist's desk. "Diane, is there a going-away party planned for Stephanie? So the residents can tell her good-bye?"

"You know?" Diane looked up over the top of her glasses.

"Yes. Oscar told me."

"What else did he tell you?"

"That my last day is Monday, and that you'll be taking over all my duties."

"Not all the duties. He said I don't have to do the newsletter."

Was that what all her angst had been over? The newsletter?

"Would you like help with the newsletter, with the issue you're working on?" Charlotte leaned toward the woman. "I'd be happy to finish it."

"Really?"

"Sure. And if needed, I could help with it as a volunteer."

"That would be great," Diane said and then smiled, the most genuine smile Charlotte had seen yet on her.

"Back to Stephanie's party," Charlotte said.

"Oh, yeah. She doesn't want one. She said it would be too sad."

"Oh."

"She said the tea was like a going-away party."

Charlotte nodded. "One more thing. Christopher's class is coming over for a Wii tournament on Tuesday."

"And that will be the last day of playing the Wii here," Diane said. "Remember, it belongs to Stephanie."

All sorts of things were changing at Bedford Gardens.

CHARLOTTE SLOWED HER FORD FOCUS as she neared the turn to Arielle's house. "Are you going to the game tonight?" Arielle asked Emily.

"Maybe, if Sam goes."

Charlotte stopped the car and Arielle thanked her for the ride. "See you at the game, if you go," Arielle said to Emily and then thanked Charlotte for the ride and told Christopher good-bye. He grunted from the back seat; stopping by the nursing home after school made for a long day for him.

Charlotte would miss spending time with Arielle at Bedford Gardens, and the sad thing was if she and Sam didn't work through their differences, they wouldn't be seeing Arielle much at all, unless she and Emily forged more of a friendship.

"What are you doing in art now that you're done with your project?" Charlotte asked Emily.

"Well, first I have to give a report Monday on what I did at the nursing home. I'm going to e-mail the photos I took on my phone to myself and show them in class. On Ms. Carey's laptop."

Charlotte nodded, as if she knew what Emily was talking about.

"Then I'm going to get started on a fashion-design line."

"Really?" Charlotte said.

"Hey, does Christopher still have the copy of the photo of Ruth?"

"Yes." She was going to give the pictures back to Red and Ruth on Monday.

"I want to look at it again. I was thinking about copying some of the lines from her skirt for a dress idea."

"Nice." Charlotte said. She'd always liked the full skirts of the fifties and early sixties.

"And I was thinking about copying the photo and doing a frame for Ruth. Since she didn't do one. What do you think?"

Charlotte nodded but she wasn't sure. Ruth had been acting so odd lately. Honestly, she didn't seem to want to have a photo of herself outside her door.

"Is it okay if I go to the game?" Emily asked.

"Sure, once your chores are done—and after you pick a bucket of plums." Charlotte was storing a bucket at a time in the basement. She would make plum preserves first chance she had, which would be much sooner than she'd thought an hour ago.

Chapter Twenty-Three

Hey, Pete, I didn't know, okay?" Sam held the pipe in his hand.

"We don't flood irrigate around here, okay? We turn the water off if the sprinkler is broken."

What was with him?

"You need to take more initiative," Pete said. "If you don't know what to do, come get me."

What was the difference? The crop still got water.

"Look at this," Pete said, pointing to the soybean plants around the pipe. "The water flattened them."

"Yeah, but they'll perk back up."

"Maybe not," Pete said.

"But they're only a few plants."

"Hey," Pete said. "It adds up. I'm just telling you, you gotta take initiative when you're a farmer." He stopped and rubbed his chin. "Actually, if you want to succeed at anything, you need to take initiative."

Initiative. He sounded like Grandpa. And Grandma. And Arielle. And Ruth too. As Uncle Pete turned toward his truck, Sam kicked at the wheel of the irrigation pipe and then stepped back in pain. Why couldn't he do anything right?

He followed Pete to the truck and climbed in.

"Going to the game tonight?" Uncle Pete asked.

Sam shrugged.

"So what's up with you and Arielle?"

"Nothing," Sam muttered.

"Nothing, as in *nothing*, or nothing as in *absolutely* nothing?"

"Just nothing."

"So she's annoyed with you, right?"

Sam slumped down in the seat. "Probably."

"And that's why you're not going to the game?"

Sam shook his head. "I was thinking about doing some research online, about colleges."

"Now you're talking," Pete turned onto the highway. "What colleges?"

Sam turned his face toward the window and didn't answer. He couldn't think that far. And it probably wouldn't do any good anyway, since apparently his grades weren't that good. It probably wouldn't even make a difference if he talked to Mr. Santos or not.

Pete turned onto the highway. "When are those soccer tryouts?"

"Tuesday."

Pete snorted. "Nothing like waiting until the last minute."

AS SAM CLIMBED DOWN from Uncle Pete's truck, Emily hurried over from the barn. "Sam, are you going to the game?" she called out.

"Nope."

"How come?" Emily reached him. "Arielle is going to be there."

Sam started toward the back door. "I have stuff to do tonight."

"Like . . . ?" Emily asked, following him closely. "What? Update your Facebook page?"

He shook his head.

"Well, what else do you have to do?"

"None of your business."

"Make a list of possible colleges," Uncle Pete said, following them toward the house.

Emily turned. "Are *you* going to the game?"

"I don't think so."

"Miss Simons will be there, probably."

Sam started to jog, relieved that Emily was hounding Uncle Pete instead of him, and slipped into the house.

A couple of minutes later he was seated at the computer, Googling San Diego State University. Grandpa hadn't said his grades had to be good enough for college—just that he had to talk to Mr. Santos and gather information. His parents had planned to go to San Diego State when they moved to California—at least that was the story—but it didn't seem very realistic considering they had a baby on the way and then another one two years later.

He clicked onto the Web site and read the first blurb on the site: "SDSU, with its diverse faculty and myriad academic programs, offers—" And then he tuned out. *Diverse*, compared to Bedford, sounded great. But the word *academic* stopped him. It didn't sound like the surfer school he was imagining. He clicked on the PROSPECTIVE STUDENTS button and there was a white mission-style building with an arched entrance. There was a VIRTUAL TOUR button, but he decided against clicking it. That would only make him homesick.

If his grades happened to be good enough, would he live in a dorm? Or an apartment? And what was the tuition? He scanned the page but couldn't find anything that suggested the costs. Out of state would be really high though. Grandma and Grandpa couldn't afford that, and neither could he, not without taking out loans up the wazoo.

What were the chances of his getting a good job after college anyway? He was always hearing about grads working as baristas, if they were lucky. And what if he wasn't college material?

Why couldn't he like farming? Suddenly Uncle Pete's life seemed like a dream, except that Sam couldn't seem to get any of it right. Not the irrigation pipes. Not the horses. He wasn't cut out for farming. Maybe he was only cut out to be a loser.

He understood Arielle looking into a college in Tennessee. There were times when he wanted to go as far away as possible. Was that how his dad had felt? Sam Googled "colleges in Australia" just as Grandma called out, "Time for dinner."

He hit the PRINT button and then clicked off the site. He'd look up some of them later. Maybe tomorrow.

He stood and headed toward the bathroom to wash up, bumping into Emily in the hallway.

"Hey, watch out," she hissed.

"Hey, want to go to the game?" he asked.

"I thought you had better things to do." She stopped.

"I already did them." He might as well go to the game. Hanging around here wasn't going to do him any good.

SAM STOOD AT THE EDGE of the football field and scanned the bleachers. Emily was hurrying up the steps to sit by Ashley, and there was Arielle's friend Halley, but no Arielle. Emily probably didn't know for sure that Arielle was going to be at the game; she was probably just assuming she would be, like Emily assumed everything else.

"Hey, up here." Jake was waving his arms from the very top bench of the bleachers.

Sam started up the stairs slowly. He shouldn't have come to the game. Chances were if he was sitting with Jake, and Arielle showed up after all, he was going to say something stupid, something more for her to get mad about. He reached the top and sat beside his friend. "Hey, where's Paul?"

"On his way," Jake said. "Hey, where's your girlfriend?"

Sam rolled his eyes. "Not."

"Yeah." Jake elbowed him. "That's what I hear too."

Sam sat with his chin in his hands through the first quarter. Bedford was ahead by a touchdown when Uncle Pete, who had cleaned up and had on a pair of dark jeans that Sam hadn't seen before and a button-up-the-front shirt, showed up. He didn't look around for Sam or anything, just plopped himself down on a bench at the bottom of the bleachers. A minute later Miss Simons arrived. She smiled a really big smile when she saw Uncle Pete, and then she sat down beside him.

Jake nudged him again. "Look," he said.

Paul had just turned the corner in front of the bleachers. He was talking to Arielle. He stopped and let her go ahead of him, and then he followed her as she made her way to sit beside Halley. Paul sat down right beside Arielle.

Jake guffawed. "Well, isn't he the mover."

Sam concentrated on not groaning.

At halftime he texted Emily: "Let's go."

"NO," she texted back.

"Yes," he shot back.

"I'll get a ride with Uncle Pete," was her response. She made her way over to their uncle, bumping into people and smiling as she excused herself. She sat beside him for a minute, talking, and then Uncle Pete said something to Miss Simons and she shrugged and Uncle Pete spoke to Emily again.

Emily stood and turned around, looked up at Sam, and gave him a thumbs-up. He nodded and then told Jake, "I'm out of here."

"Where ya going?"

"Home."

Sam stood and stole another look at Arielle. Paul had grabbed her sweatshirt and had draped it over his head, pretending he had long hair. Well, at least Sam hadn't said anything stupid to her tonight. He really didn't want to walk down the bleachers, to draw attention to himself. He didn't want everyone to know he was all alone while Paul sat next to Arielle, even if it was only as friends. He had spent a lot of time with her this summer and he thought they got along really well together. He liked being with her. He liked that she was so honest and knew so much about how things worked, like talking to the counselor and helping Red with his paperwork. She was smart like that, about dealing with life and doing the right thing. He hadn't meant to hurt her feelings, but he didn't know how to tell her that.

He looked over his shoulder. It wasn't that much of a drop to the ground from the bleachers. He shimmied over the top and lowered his body down, first holding on to the backrest and then lowering his hands, one by one, to the back edge of the bench.

"What are you doing?" Jake asked, turning around.

"Leaving." Sam dropped down, landing on his feet, his knees buckling, and then springing to his feet.

Jake stood and leaned against the backrest. "Sam," he yelled in mock horror. "Are you okay? Did you hurt yourself?"

"Shut up," Sam called up, imagining everyone hearing—Emily and Uncle Pete and, of course, Arielle. He hurried toward the gate but turned just before he exited. Arielle stood at the corner of the bleachers, watching him go. For a minute he thought he would go back to her, but then he raised his hand and waved, barely, and then scurried through the gate to his car.

Chapter Twenty-Four

Charlotte pulled the covers up around Christopher's chin after she had finished praying with him. "Good night, sweetie," she said. How long had it been since she'd tucked him in? She knew, from when her own kids were little, that the time would soon come when Christopher stayed up later than she did. She wouldn't always be able to tuck him in. She needed to do it every night for as long as she could.

"Grandma," he said as she stood.

She turned toward him.

"What's going to happen when you're old?"

"What do you mean?"

"Will you live at Bedford Gardens?"

"We'll see," she answered. "Grandpa's mother lived here on the farm until she died. Who knows? Maybe Grandpa and I will end up moving into Pete's apartment someday."

Christopher shook his head. "Nah. Grandpa couldn't live without his chair."

"We'd take his chair with us," Charlotte said, and then smiled. "But that's a long way away, Christopher. You'll be off to college by then."

His eyes got big. "That is a long time from now." He scrunched down farther under the covers.

"Yes, indeed," Charlotte answered, but then she winced. To Christopher it was a long time, but for her the next seven years would go by in a flash. She bent down and kissed his forehead again and then headed down the stairs. The back door slammed. It was early for the kids to be home from the game. As she reached the bottom stair, Sam turned from the hallway to the family room.

"Home already?" she asked.

"Yep."

"Where's Emily?"

"She's coming with Uncle Pete."

"Oh." Charlotte hadn't realized Pete had gone in to the game.

"Who won?"

"We were ahead when I left." Sam ducked into the family room and Charlotte stood in the doorway. He slumped into the computer chair and twirled around.

She couldn't help but be worried about him. He'd been so quiet and moody lately. He said he wanted to play soccer, but he wasn't following through on looking into colleges, and he'd left the football game early. What high schooler did that?

"Why did you come home so soon?" Charlotte took a step into the family room.

Sam shrugged without turning around.

"Did anything happen?"

"I was bored, that's all." He logged on to the computer.

Charlotte wanted to ask if he had talked to the office

ladies about when Mr. Santos would be back, but she stepped from the room instead. She had promised herself she wouldn't nag Sam. It was up to him to do what he needed to do.

She headed down the hall to her bedroom. Bob must already be in bed. She wished he would tell her good night; she hated going to bed and already having him asleep. She eased open their door and peered at the bed, straining to see from the light in the hallway. The bed was empty. Where was Bob?

She padded back up the hall, through the kitchen, and to the back door, stepping out into the yard. Toby hurried toward her, her tail wagging. "Have you seen Grandpa?" Charlotte asked. Toby barked and nudged her head against Charlotte's hand.

The half moon hung in the night sky above the barn and the stars were coming out, one by one. The shed door was closed and the lights were off, and Bob's pickup was parked by the barn.

A cow mooed in the distance, and Toby nuzzled her hand again. Maybe Bob was on the front porch. She made her way around the side of the house, walking on the grass that needed to be watered. Tomorrow would be a day of chores—tending to the yard and garden. She needed to pull out her canning jars too and get started on the tomatoes that were all quickly ripening on the vine in the garden. She would can tomatoes and make plum preserves starting next Wednesday, after her last day at Bedford Gardens. She rounded the house. The porch light was off. She started up the steps.

"Hi," Bob said from the Adirondack chair in the corner of the porch.

"There you are." Charlotte pulled the second chair closer to his and sat down.

"Nice night, huh?" Bob tilted his head.

"How long have you been out here?" Charlotte asked.

"An hour or so, since dusk."

Charlotte thought he'd been asleep in his chair inside the whole time. "I talked to Oscar Smith today," she said.

"And . . . ?"

"Monday, actually Tuesday, is my last day." She expected him to say good or it's about time, but he didn't.

"Will you miss it, Char?"

"I thought I'd volunteer one day a week, but earlier in the day. Not so close to dinnertime."

He was silent. Maybe he'd gone to sleep.

The porch light turned on and Sam stuck his head out the door. "What are you guys doing?" he asked.

"Just talking," Charlotte answered but that wasn't really true. "Just being."

Sam wrinkled his nose. "Well, I'm going to go listen to some music and then go to bed."

"Son, we'll need your help tomorrow. Down in the home quarter."

Sam nodded but he didn't look very enthusiastic.

"And we have a lot of chores to catch up on around the house and yard too," Charlotte added.

Sam said a quick good night and ducked back into the house, probably afraid of what else they might say.

Charlotte added cleaning out the refrigerator to her

mental to-do list. One thing she realized from working was just how much there really was to do around the house. When she was working at it day by day, she wasn't as aware of it. It was so routine, so ingrained into who she was. But when she didn't have afternoons to keep up with things, it had all started to pile up.

Still, she would miss working at Bedford Gardens. It had given her extra purpose. And, quite honestly, a feeling of accomplishment, but the experience had made her thankful for the life she had too. If she had had a career, she would be retiring about now. As it was, she was still active, still needed, still in the middle of her game. She just hoped volunteering would be as fulfilling as working there had been.

"Well, you've done a good thing, Char." Bob leaned forward in the chair.

"It's been good for me," she said. She started to say she would miss it, but before she could Bob announced that he was off to bed and asked if she was coming.

Annoyed, Charlotte answered, "I'll come in after Emily gets home." Why couldn't he stay up for half an hour more?

Bob patted her hand as he walked by, but then to her surprise he came back and sat down again. "Char," he said, "I'm sorry I've been grumpy the last few weeks. I guess I was used to having you around for all those years. And then when the kids came I had to adjust to you being busy. And then when you started at Bedford Gardens it felt like too much, even though I knew it was temporary."

Charlotte exhaled. She couldn't remember the last time Bob had apologized.

"It's really made me appreciative of everything you do around here. I'd been taking it for granted, and I'm sorry about that. I realized that last night." Without waiting for her to answer, he headed back to the front door and banged through the screen.

Charlotte stayed put in the chair. Well, that was something, to have Bob appreciate what she did on the farm. She began thinking of all the mechanical work he did and the farming and even hanging out with Christopher after school.

And she appreciated how firm Bob was with Sam. He didn't get emotional or threaten or nag. He just stated the way things were going to be and left it at that. That was the thing with Bob. He didn't overthink things or question his own motives; he stood his ground.

Pete's pickup pulled into the driveway, and he must have seen Charlotte sitting on the porch because he honked as he passed the house. A minute later, Emily came prancing around the side yard.

"Hi, Grandma." She bounded up the stairs, her blonde ponytail sashaying from side to side. "We won." Emily sat down in the chair Bob had vacated. "How are things around here?"

"Fine," Charlotte answered. "Christopher is in bed and Sam is up in his room."

"Already?" Emily wrinkled her nose. "He's been acting so weird lately."

Pete opened the front door. "Looks like Sam forgot something in the printer." He held up a piece of paper.

"What is it?"

"A list of colleges. In Australia."

Charlotte shook her head. She wanted to laugh, but it wasn't funny. Just maybe, though, it was a start.

SATURDAY MORNING, as Charlotte pulled containers of leftover food from the refrigerator, the phone rang. She waited for three rings, hoping Emily would get it, but then she remembered that Emily was out in the barn, mucking out the stalls.

Charlotte snatched up the phone and was surprised to find out it was Ruth.

"Dear," she said, "do you have a little extra time today? I'd love to have a chat after all."

When Charlotte was on a cleaning binge, she hated to be distracted by anything; on the other hand, she didn't think Ruth would ask to see her unless it was really important. "Is everything all right?"

"Oh, yes." Ruth paused. "It's just that I'm hoping for some advice from you." She paused again. "Actually, I've just made a huge decision and I need someone—someone sane—to tell me if I've done the right thing or not."

Charlotte laughed. "Oh, I'm hardly the one for you to talk with then."

"Oh, no," Ruth said. "You are the only one for me to talk with."

Charlotte agreed to come into town in the afternoon.

"We'll have tea then," Ruth said.

"I'll bring the cookies." Charlotte hung up, feeling disconcerted. What was up with Ruth?

RED WAS AT HIS USUAL POST at the top of the stairs when Charlotte arrived.

"I'm missing a piece to the puzzle," he said, pointing to the picture of the Irish village. "After all that work." He stood. "What are you doing here on a Saturday afternoon?"

"I'm visiting Ruth."

"Really?" Red leaned on his cane. "She hasn't been out of her room in days."

Charlotte hurried on down the hall, not wanting to talk with Red about Ruth. Just as she knocked, Ruth's door swung open. "Oh, do come in," she said. Behind her were boxes and more boxes, and her walls were bare, not a painting left in sight.

Charlotte sank down onto the sofa, and Ruth sat beside her, her hands folded over her apron.

"Ruth, what's going on?"

"I'm leaving Bedford."

"Where are you going?"

Ruth's eyes sparkled. "Across the pond."

"Pardon?"

"I'm going home." Ruth took Charlotte's hand in hers.

"Ruth, what are you talking about?"

The old woman sighed. "You know, I've been e-mailing back and forth with my nephew, and he's offered me the flat on the first level of his house. It's my father's old home, actually. And he's arranging for assistance for me, so I won't be dependent on him and his wife. I'll have a woman who comes in to clean and cook and help with paperwork and errands. That sort of thing." She paused and exhaled slowly. "I've decided I want to live by family after all these years; I want to go home."

"What about your health?"

"They have doctors in England, although probably not as good as Dr. Carr." Ruth chuckled.

"And what about traveling?" Charlotte asked.

"I suppose it's a bit of a risk, but I'll take it. My nephew is hiring an escort to fly with me from New York, for the trans-Atlantic flight. I cannot explain the urge I have to go home. It's primordial, really."

"Have you told people here?" Charlotte knew she hadn't, at least not Red.

Ruth nodded. "I've told Oscar Smith and given him my notice, so to speak. And Stephanie has offered to give me a ride to Omaha, to the airport. I'll have some of my things shipped, but I'll have to leave most of them. I'm going to donate my china to Bedford Gardens."

"What about your condo in Seattle?"

"It's on the market. If it doesn't sell, the rent will go toward my estate, to my nephew and his family." Ruth's eyes filled with tears. "I do hope I have enough time to get properly acquainted with them."

"What did you want to ask me?" Charlotte squeezed Ruth's hand. It seemed she had everything figured out.

"Do you think I'm crazy?"

Charlotte shook her head. It was hard to speak. She would miss the woman dearly. "I admire you," she managed to say.

The kettle whistled and Ruth rose. Charlotte followed her into the tiny kitchen. "Mostly," Ruth said as she poured the boiling water into the teapot, "I want you to know how much I've appreciated getting to know you and your grandchildren. I would love to tell them good-bye before I go. Would that be possible?"

"Definitely," Charlotte said. "In fact, Christopher's class is coming on Tuesday for a Wii tournament with the residents. I didn't get a chance to tell you."

"Oh, perfect," Ruth said, fitting the tea cozy over the pot. "I'll challenge them all to a round of golf."

"When do you leave?"

"Wednesday." Ruth took cups from the cupboard. "I fly out early, to New York and then on to London."

"Now," Ruth said, "after having told you, I think I have the gumption to tell Red."

Charlotte didn't need to say it would break the poor man's heart. Ruth already knew that.

Chapter Twenty-Five

Monday morning before first period, Sam knocked on Mr. Santos's door, first tentatively and then more aggressively. He tried the doorknob. It was locked. He pulled his foot back to kick the door but first glanced down the hall. Arielle and Halley turned the corner and were walking toward him, but maybe they hadn't seen him. He ducked his head and turned the opposite way.

Arielle was right. He did care too much about what other people thought; he even cared too much about what the lady in the office said. Did he really want to play soccer, no matter what?

He took a deep breath and headed down the hall, slipping through the doorway of the office. The younger secretary, not the one who had been mean to him the week before, asked if she could help him. He cleared his throat. "Is Mr. Santos in today?"

She smiled at him. "He'll probably be in this afternoon. He had a doctor's appointment this morning."

"Thanks," Sam said.

"What do you need?" the woman asked. "I've been covering for him." Maybe she didn't realize how bad his grades were.

"Information on colleges."

"Which ones?" she asked. Would Grandma and Grandpa be okay with him talking to the school secretary instead of Mr. Santos?

Sam pulled his list from his back pocket.

"Have you checked for information online?"

Sam said yes, but added that he needed to find out what Mr. Santos knew about the colleges and get an idea of costs and possible financial aid.

"Come on down," the secretary said. "Let's see what I can find in his files."

Sam followed her down the hall, passing Arielle and Halley, who were absorbed in conversation, and into Mr. Santos's office. Posters from colleges covered the walls. He hadn't remembered that from before. *Notre Dame. Duke. Harvard.* Sam wanted to laugh. He wouldn't go to a place like that in a million years.

The secretary opened the drawer to Mr. Santos's desk. "Here's a basic worksheet to help you think through what kind of college you're interested in. Community college. University. State. Out of state. That sort of thing. And here's a financial worksheet for you to do with your, um, grandparents to help figure that part out."

Sam scanned the bookcase and the college catalogs that filled it.

"You can look for catalogs you're interested in; you just have to check them out."

Sam found the San Diego State University catalog and pulled it from the bookcase. And the University of Nebraska because there were several copies. The Harding State catalog was gone though.

The secretary looked at the checkout list on Mr. Santos's desk. "Arielle Friesen has that one," she said. "Ask her if she's done with it."

Sam nodded, but there was no way he'd ask Arielle for anything. Not now.

"If you have any specific questions for Mr. Santos, check in this afternoon," the secretary said as they left the office.

"Thank you," Sam answered as she locked the door behind him. He had everything he needed, everything to satisfy Grandma and Grandpa, at least, to make them think he was serious about looking at colleges.

But he still had one more question. One for Mr. Santos.

SAM SLUMPED INTO HIS CHAIR in yearbook class just as the bell rang; a second later Jake fell into the chair next to Sam's. "Hey," Jake said, "want to skate after school?"

Sam shook his head. "Nah, I'm busy."

"How about tomorrow?"

Sam shook his head.

Arielle must have overheard Jake because she butted in and asked Sam if he was going to Bedford Gardens tomorrow for the Wii tournament.

"The what?" Jake asked and then hooted.

"The Wii tournament," Arielle said without fanfare. "Sam's little brother Christopher's class is going to play against the residents."

"That sounds like the most boring—"

"Actually," Sam interrupted, "I hope to be in Harding at soccer tryouts."

"Cool," Arielle said.

"You're ditching me for soccer?" Jake crossed his arms.

Sam smiled. "And if it wasn't for soccer, I'd be at Bedford Gardens for the tournament, 'cuz that sounds like a lot of fun." Sam turned toward Arielle as he spoke.

"So did you talk to Mr. Santos?"

"Nah. The secretary helped me."

"He's in his office now. I bet you could get a hall pass."

Sam sat up straight. All he had to do was ask.

"So why are you ditching me today?" Jake asked.

"I have to sign up for soccer tryouts. Online. By five o'clock."

"When did you get so responsible?" Jake crossed his arms.

Sam stood.

A minute later Sam was knocking on Mr. Santos's office door. "Come in," said a weak voice.

Sam opened the door, and there sat Mr. Santos, his face pale and thin.

"Ah, Sam," he said, "I saw that you stopped by this morning. What can I do for you? Do you need some more information?"

Sam sat down across the desk from the counselor. "I think I have what I need. I just have a question—um, about my grades."

"Yes?"

"I'm just wondering if my grades are good enough—you know, to get into college." What he really wanted to ask was if Mr. Santos thought he was too big of a loser to get into college, but framing the question that way would probably get him on a watch-this-kid-closely list.

"Depends on what college." Mr. Santos leaned forward. "Harvard," he nodded toward the poster, "no. A community college, yes. Harding State, maybe. But," he sat up straight, "it depends on how you do on your SATs and in your classes this year."

Sam crossed his arms.

"It's up to you, Sam."

Sam stood. It wasn't a particularly hopeful answer, but it didn't sound hopeless either. Sam thanked Mr. Santos and started for the door but then turned. "Hey, I'm sorry you've been sick."

"Thanks," Mr. Santos said. "So am I—and sorry that I haven't been around to help you and the other students. I was surprised that you went to the office for help, actually. Pleasantly surprised."

The words hung in Sam's brain as he walked back to yearbook class. *Pleasantly surprised*. So was he.

"HEY, I NEED THE COMPUTER," Sam said to Emily. "Now." They'd only been home for three minutes. How could she get on the computer so fast?

"Wait your turn."

"No, I have a deadline. I need it now."

"A deadline." She spun around in the chair, a look of mock horror on her face. "Well, if it's due tomorrow, you'll have plenty of time to work on it this evening." She spun back around and clicked on a bookmarked site. A fashion Web site appeared.

Sam groaned. "Come on, Em. This is really important."

"Wait," Emily hissed.

"Em!" he shouted.

"Hush, you're going to wake Grandpa."

Sam grabbed the chair and yanked her backward. "Where's Grandma?"

"At Bedford Gardens, remember? It's her last day, except for the tournament tomorrow."

"Her last day?"

"Yeah, she's probably spending it with Ruth."

"With Ruth? Why?" Was something wrong with Ruth?

"Yeah. Did you forget that Ruth is moving back to England?"

"What?" No one had told him that.

"Grandma told us at dinner on Saturday night. What's with you?"

What was with him? He glanced at the clock. Saturday night. Was that when he was out helping Pete and got into dinner late? It seemed like Grandma was always doing that, telling something to the family but forgetting to tell whoever wasn't present. Wow, Ruth was going to England. She'd probably get to see Chelsea play, live.

He glanced at the clock above the TV. Four o'clock. He had an hour—he needed to get online *now*. What if the site crashed? Or there were some other problems?

"Come on, Em. I need to sign up for tryouts."

"Tryouts? But you didn't do what Grandma and Grandpa told you to."

"Actually, I did. I have all the information in my backpack."

"Really?"

He started to pull out the catalogs and handouts.

"I believe you," Emily said, "really." She clicked off the fashion site. "You have ten minutes, max. That's it." She stood.

Sam sank into the chair and clicked onto the Harding Soccer Club site and went straight to the tryouts form. He quickly filled in his name and information and hit send. A notice popped up that he hadn't paid. Paid? He hit the back button and reread the application. There at the bottom was a pay button. It cost forty dollars to try out. His hand fell away from the mouse. Now what? He stared at the screen for a minute.

"Are you done?" Emily asked, sashaying back into the room, an apple in her hand.

"Nope." Sam clicked off the site.

"What are you doing?" she asked and then took a bite of the apple.

He shrugged. He didn't want to talk about it.

"Sam," Emily wailed, "why did you do that?"

"I have to pay—and I don't have the money." How could he have been so stupid not to have read that part?

"Well, ask Grandpa. Maybe he'll help you. Or Pete—he's out back."

"I need a credit card."

Emily threw up one hand. "Grandpa has a credit card. Pete might."

Sam shook his head. He'd never seen Pete use a card, just a debit card, and he could only imagine the lecture Grandpa would give him.

"It doesn't matter," Sam said.

"You are such a loser," Emily said. She looked like she

was ready to throw the half-eaten apple at him. "You want this, right? And here you are, having come this far, ready to let it go."

Sam shook his head.

"No, it's true." Emily was squeezing the apple. "That's the worst kind of loser."

Grandpa stirred again and then opened his eyes. "What's going on?"

"Sam needs to pay for tryouts," Emily sneered at her brother as she spoke.

"Tryouts. What are you up to, son?" Grandpa sat up straight.

"I talked with Mr. Santos today," Sam said. "And I got the college info." He exhaled and then spoke. "But I didn't notice that I need to pay to do tryouts."

"What in the world . . . ?" Grandpa said. As he stood and started over toward the computer, Emily left the room.

Sam pointed to the screen. "Forty bucks," he said.

Grandpa whistled. "Have you spoken to your grandmother about all this?"

"She's at the nursing home."

Grandpa sat down on the couch. "Show me what you found out from the counselor."

"I only have until five PM to register," Sam said.

"Show me." Grandpa pulled his reading glasses from his head and positioned them on his face.

Sam pulled the catalogs and worksheets from his backpack.

"What college are you interested in?" Grandpa asked.

"It depends on my SATs and grades—and finances," Sam answered.

Grandpa nodded, turning over the San Diego State catalog in his hands. "And that's why your grades and SATs are so important."

Sam agreed, but inside he questioned how much control he had over his SATs. The whole college thing felt like such a black hole.

"It's step by step, son," Grandpa said. "You get the information, take your SATs, get good grades, apply to colleges, pray, and see what happens."

Not much would happen if he didn't have the money for college; that was for sure.

"How about Harding?" Grandpa put down the San Diego State catalog. "Do you think you could get a soccer scholarship?"

Sam sighed. "I haven't played high school soccer for two years. I don't know—I guess I might have a better idea if I make it to tryouts." He looked at the clock. It was four fifteen.

"So how do you pay? Over the computer?"

"We have to use a credit card."

"A card?" Grandpa looked puzzled. "Is that safe?"

Sam assured him it was.

Grandpa looked befuddled and started patting his back pocket. Then he stood and started down the hall. Sam put his head in his hands. He was doomed. Just as Grandpa came back with his open billfold, Emily dragged Uncle Pete into the room, followed by Christopher.

"Grandma's the one who keeps our credit card," Grandpa said. "I'm sorry, Sam."

"I'll pay with mine," Uncle Pete said. "As long as someone pays me back."

"Sam can pay you from the money he earns at the airport," Grandpa said.

Sam spun around in the chair. "But what if I make the team? That's another two hundred bucks. And with practices and games I don't know how much time I'd have left over to work."

"Well, you'll have to figure out how to juggle it all. You don't want to quit your job, even if it's only a few hours a week," Grandpa said.

Pete hunched over the computer, typed in his card info, and hit the PAY button.

Chapter Twenty-Six

Charlotte stood in the middle of the activity room and turned around slowly, taking in the worn couches, dingy walls, and folding chairs. She was done with her career at Bedford Gardens. Today was the beginning of her work as a volunteer.

She turned on the TV and clicked onto the game setting and then turned on the Wii. Twelve students were coming. Four would play each game—bowling, golf, and baseball. The residents began gathering in the room. First Aggie wheeled in with a group of ladies—bowlers—following her. Then Red walked in, leaning heavily against his cane.

"How are you?" Charlotte asked.

"Just fine," Red answered. "I couldn't be better."

When Arielle arrived a minute later, Charlotte nodded toward Red, and the young woman went over and sat beside him. In another minute Arielle was smiling and Red was laughing out loud. Charlotte smiled to herself. Arielle definitely had a touch.

Christopher's newspaper class arrived next, led by Miss Luka. Charlotte decided to start with bowling.

Christopher's classmates won the game when all the scores were totaled, although Betty was the overall top scorer. She smiled in triumph at the acknowledgment. Next up was baseball, with Red pitching.

Charlotte stepped into the hall. Where was Ruth?

"Ninety-five miles an hour," Red hooted. "That's the fastest I've ever pitched in my life." He struck out a second player.

Miss Luka approached Charlotte at the doorway. "What a wonderful experience for the students," she said. "Actually, it's good for me too. I've always dreaded getting old." She laughed. "Even though it's years away for me. But this doesn't look so bad."

Charlotte patted the young woman's shoulder. She wanted to tell her it would all come much faster than she could ever imagine. The decades would speed by and before she knew it she would be in her sixties. But Charlotte bit her tongue and didn't say anything at all because just then Ruth slipped through the doorway.

"Sorry to be late, deary," Ruth said. "I'm at the end of my tether, I'm afraid. I almost didn't come at all."

Charlotte put an arm around her and squeezed.

Ruth leaned her head against Charlotte's shoulder. "I'm afraid I've hurt Red deeply." She stared at him, pitching in the middle of the room, his eyes intent on the TV, as she spoke. "He hasn't spoken to me since Saturday."

"Oh dear," Charlotte said.

"Oh dear is right." Ruth tried to smile. "Falling for an older woman was a foolish thing for him to do. He has years ahead of him; he needs to find someone his own age."

Charlotte couldn't imagine.

"In fact, I encouraged him to do some traveling of his own. He has a son in Florida he should visit. Can't you imagine Red down there?" Ruth smiled. "Just think how many dance partners he would have." She continued walking, and then stopped abruptly beside Christopher, who sat on the couch. "I hear you've challenged me," she said, ruffling his hair.

Christopher smiled up at her, flashing his dimples, but then his face fell. "I hear you're moving."

"Hush," she said. "Not now. Now is the time for fun."

Red heard her voice and turned. A look of pain spread over his face. Ruth waved a hand at him, a get-back-to-business gesture, and he refocused on his game.

After baseball, Red sat back down next to Arielle and Ruth and Christopher took their places. Charlotte wandered around the room, chatting with both residents and students, but when she overheard Red talking to Arielle about Florida, she stopped within hearing distance.

"My son lives in Orlando; he works for Disney," Red was saying.

"Any grandkids?" Arielle asked.

"Two. Ten and eight. Little girls."

"That sounds like a wonderful trip," Arielle said.

"WHERE'D YOU LEARN to play soccer, Bedford boy? A cow pasture?" the player in the Man U jersey jeered as his shoulder crashed into Sam.

Sam held his own, making his way around the player

and then finding an open spot, ready for the pass. He waved his arm, trying to signal his teammate with the ball that he was open, but the guy passed it the other way and it was easily intercepted by the other team. Sam turned quickly, defending the Man U guy as the pass came his way. Sam intercepted it and, although he was tempted to hang on to the ball and try to dribble it down the field for a shot of his own, he passed it. He knew he'd never make the team if he didn't look like a team player, even though it didn't come naturally to him.

"Shoot!" he yelled as the ball sailed to the foot of his teammate. The player turned and lobbed the ball high. It sailed in just under the crossbar for a goal.

But as they ran back to their side of the field for the kick-off, none of his teammates high-fived him for the assist; they only swarmed the shooter for the goal.

"Good job, Sam!" It was number 8 from the Harding State soccer team, one of the players he'd met in Bedford.

"Lucky break," yelled the opposing player wearing the Man U jersey. That was how the entire scrimmage, the entire tryout, went. At the end, Sam dropped his water bottle and ball into his bag and zipped it quickly.

What did it matter that he'd passed the ball? None of his teammates had gone out of their way to pass to him.

"I'll call everyone ASAP," the coach was saying. The other players were laughing and joking. Obviously they all knew each other and had played together for years. What a waste of forty bucks, and now he had to pay Pete back.

As he headed toward his car, he heard the Harding State soccer player call out his name. Sam turned. The player, wearing a snazzy Nike warm-up suit, jogged toward him. "Good tryout," he said.

Sam shrugged.

"I know, I know," the guy said. "They hardly passed you the ball. Believe me, the coach saw that. He also saw every time you got the ball, you made the right move. You're a smart player."

"Thanks," Sam said.

Sam swiped the sweat off his forehead with the back of his hand. He had no idea what to say to the guy. There was no way he was going to make the team.

He accelerated toward Bedford at the Harding city limits. Why had he even gone to the tryouts? It had been such a hassle to get the college information. Why had he bothered? Right now he wished he were at Bedford Gardens, hanging out with Christopher and Ruth and Ari. She'd actually been nice to him today. Too bad they didn't have FIFA soccer for the Wii at the Gardens. It would be a blast to play Ruth—she'd probably beat him though.

It was five o'clock. Maybe they were all still there. He'd stop by. He could at least tell Ruth good-bye, if nothing else.

Chapter Twenty-Seven

Charlotte boxed up the Wii. Stephanie would pick it up the next day when she picked up Ruth. No more bowling, baseball, or golf, unless Oscar broke down and bought one. It would be back to movie and popcorn nights and cribbage and pinochle.

All the students had left except for Christopher. He and Arielle were helping Red look for the missing piece to his puzzle, and Ruth and Emily, who had walked over after school, were chatting with Aggie in the lobby.

Charlotte glanced at her watch. *Five thirty*. Time for the residents to eat and time for her, Emily, and Christopher to get home.

She carried the box toward the stairs as a car backfired in the parking lot.

"That sounds like Sam," Christopher said.

Charlotte shook her head. "He's in Harding." But she was wrong. Here came Sam through the front door, dressed in a jersey, shorts, and flip-flops.

"Sam," Ruth called out, "did you make the team?"

Sam shook his head. "I don't think so." He walked over to her side. "I came to tell you good-bye."

Charlotte started down the stairs followed by Christopher, Arielle, and Red.

"I'll let you know when I go to a Chelsea game," Ruth said. "So you can cheer me on."

Sam smiled. "Sounds good."

"Sam," Diane called out from the desk, "your grandpa's on the phone."

Charlotte picked up her pace across the lobby. Why would Bob want to talk to Sam?

He picked up the phone and listened for a minute. Then he said, "Pardon?" Sam listened again and then blurted out, "Are you kidding?" and then, "Grandpa, are you sure? Maybe he said I *didn't* make the team?"

Another pause.

"Practice starts on Monday? Is that what you said?"

Arielle and Emily squealed in unison, and Ruth said, "He made the team!"

"Okay, okay. We'll be home right away," Sam said. "I'll tell Grandma." Sam hung up the phone. "Grandpa said he misses you and he hopes you'll be home soon." Then he broke out in a smile. "And, yes, I made the team."

A cheer went up.

"Stay right here," Ruth said, and she turned and hurried up the stairs. The children said good-bye to Red, who announced he planned to go to Florida for a visit. Everyone agreed it was a wonderful idea.

Ruth returned with a scarf and presented it to Sam.

"It's her Chelsea fan scarf," Red said, smiling.

"I'll get a new one." Ruth draped it around Sam's sweaty neck.

As the children said good-bye to Ruth, Charlotte stepped back, thankful for the chance they'd had to become acquainted with her. "I have to thank all of you," Ruth said, "for a wonderful end to my summer. You've blessed me, as a family, so much that you've launched me on a new adventure." She hugged each one of them.

"Remember that God has a plan for you," Ruth said to the children. "It won't be without pain. You already know that. But He has a plan." She hugged each of them again and then turned to Red. "And He has a plan for each of us too, my friend."

He bowed slightly. "I know, I know." And then he took her frail hand and kissed it tenderly. "Thank you," he whispered.

"Time to eat!" the cook called out from the entrance to the dining room. "Ruth, I made bread pudding for your last night here. Get yourself in here."

Ruth slipped her arm through Red's, and they trotted off toward the dining room. Ruth waved her other hand behind her. "Cheers," she called out.

"Cheers," the children answered as Charlotte herded them out the door.

"I'm going to give Arielle a ride home," Sam said.

"Can I ride along?" Emily asked.

"Sure," Arielle said.

"And me too?" Christopher added.

"Why not?" Sam answered, looking like it wasn't what he had planned but he could deal with it.

Charlotte waved to the children as she pulled out of her parking place, thankful she would have a few minutes with Bob before the grandchildren arrived home.

About the Author

Leslie Gould is the #1 bestselling and Christy-Award winning author of over forty novels. She and her husband, Peter, live in Portland, Oregon and enjoy hiking, traveling, and hanging out with their adult children and young grandson.

A Note from the Editors

We hope you enjoyed this volume in the Home to Heather Creek series, published by Guideposts. For over seventy-five years, Guideposts, a nonprofit organization, has been driven by a vision of a world filled with hope. We aspire to be the voice of a trusted friend, a friend who makes you feel more hopeful and connected.

By making a purchase from Guideposts, you join our community in touching millions of lives, inspiring them to believe that all things are possible through faith, hope, and prayer. Your continued support allows us to provide uplifting resources to those in need.

Whether through our online communities, websites, apps, or publications, we strive to inspire our audiences, bring them together, and comfort, uplift, entertain, and guide them.

To learn more, please go to guideposts.org.